This book is a powerful, persuasive case that the people of Christ should care about the vulnerable, including those fleeing from danger. Read this book with an open mind and a Christ-shaped conscience.

RUSSELL MOORE | President, Southern Baptist Ethics & Religious Liberty Commission

The central call of Christians is to love God and love others, and to serve the "least of these" among us. This book calls churches across America to break out of their comfort zones and renew their love of their neighbors by welcoming and serving the marginalized, the oppressed, the downtrodden, and the vulnerable—and using these opportunities to spread the gospel of Jesus Christ to new people groups through word and deed. I urge all Christians everywhere to think seriously about how they can answer that call.

CONGRESSMAN RANDY HULTGREN (IL-14) | Executive Committee, Tom Lantos Human Rights Commission, and commissioner, Helsinki Commission (Commission on Security and Cooperation in Europe)

If you are at all skeptical about how good people should respond to the refugee crisis in the world today, this book will serve to answer your questions in a fair and balanced way. If you are concerned for national security if refugees are allowed to come into the US, this is your book. If you are convinced that the US should step up to a larger role in resettlement of the displaced and oppressed, this will temper an unintentional naiveté with a realistic understanding of the challenges and the needed commitment. This book unpacks the gospel and would serve college classes and church groups alike.

SHIRLEY HOOGSTRA | President, Council for Christian Colleges & Universities

In a culture that is increasingly plunging into self-centered isolationism, the church must pour itself out on behalf of the refugees landing on her doorsteps. To fail to do so is simply to fail to be the body of Jesus Christ. Rooted in solid research and the authors' vast experience, *Seeking Refuge* both challenges and equips the church to take action in the face of the growing global crisis. A book no church can afford to be without.

BRIAN FIKKERT | Coauthor, *When Helping Hurts*, and president of The Chalmers Center at Covenant College

As the world confronts the greatest refugee crisis in recorded history, Bauman, Soerens, and Smeir argue persuasively that the church must be at the center of the solution. Biblically based, missionally minded, and informed by lots and lots of facts, *Seeking Refuge* challenges the church to step up to respond to the refugees reaching our shores with compassion, wisdom, and courage. I'd encourage every Christ follower to read this book—and then to take up its challenge.

ED STETZER | LifeWay Research

An antidote to fear…brings courage and boldness to Christ followers' hearts and behavior…prophetic challenge for these days…I was personally moved to be more like Jesus and lead the church to be the church of Jesus Christ at this time in history. The nascent voices yell loudly, but the authors are calling us to follow the "still small voice" of truth in which we experience true power in action. Guidance for these days!

JO ANNE LYON | General Superintendent, The Wesleyan Church

The refugee crisis touches nearly every community in the world, from Syria and Germany to New York and Iowa. If churches want to think biblically about this global crisis—as well as discern how to respond where they are—they couldn't do better than by reading and discussing together *Seeking Refuge*.

MARK GALLI | Editor, *Christianity Today*

The topic of refugees has become complicated, messy, and often, very contentious. As a result, it's far too tempting to dehumanize, "otherize," or altogether ignore the local and global realities of refugees. This is why I'm genuinely grateful for this book, *Seeking Refuge*. The authors have written an important and much-needed resource that acknowledges the complexities and messiness but still points us to a deeper hope that we desperately need in our world. Some will likely label this just as a book about refugees, but let me make it clear: *Seeking Refuge* is really a book about discipleship…and we're all called to grow as disciples of Christ.

EUGENE CHO | Senior Pastor, Quest Church, and author, *Overrated: Are We More in Love with the Idea of Changing the World Than Actually Changing the World?*

This book has very great prophetic value. It is a must-read for church and denominational leaders relative to this topic. We are at a crossroads. The Scriptures clearly charge us to love the stranger. While our governmental leaders are charged to be concerned about the proper processing of these refugees, the church has vital interests in this matter, namely the Great Commandment and the Great Commission.

ALEJANDRO MANDES | Director of Immigrant Mission, Evangelical Free Church of America

There is little doubt that one of the greatest tension points in our generation is the complex challenge of the refugee crisis. While the rest of the world peers into the problem through the lens of politics, economics, and cultural dilution, Bauman, Soerens, and Smeir call Christ followers to see it as an opportunity for the church to unleash the power of the gospel. In practical and persuading ways, *Seeking Refuge* offers us biblically wise counsel and effective paradigms that will bring Jesus' love and redeeming power to bear on the lives of some of the neediest people on the planet.

JOE STOWELL | President, Cornerstone University

Seeking Refuge invites all Christians in to life-changing ministries of service and justice with refugees. In opening our hearts and communities to newcomers, their lives are transformed and so too are our own. I encourage anyone who is ready to explore God's call to "welcome the stranger" to read this book.

LINDA HARTKE | President & CEO, Lutheran Immigration and Refugee Service

Much of what is being said about refugees in today's America comes from a position of fear, prejudice, or ignorance. Too often, that combination inspires a form of invincible ignorance that refuses even to consider the facts—a position no Christian can hold with gospel integrity. Through powerful stories, personal experience, a rigorous presentation of the facts, and scriptural fidelity, Bauman, Soerens, and Smeir accomplish more than merely a defense of the world's most vulnerable people. They bring truth to the rescue of Christians who would fail Jesus by refusing to make room among us for refugees.

JOSEPH CASTLEBERRY | President, Northwest University, and author, *The New Pilgrims: How Immigrants are Renewing America's Faith and Values*

Seeking Refuge arrives at a critical point of time for the church. As politicians and media seek to shape our responses to the unprecedented number of refugees around the world, the authors provide a compelling biblical basis that remind us of the nature of justice and righteousness, and that lead us to Christ-centered perspectives, compelling us to act. Moreover, their careful analyses and explanations should equip us with the knowledge and skills necessary to be the transformational agents of the Holy Spirit in the lives of refugees, among our congregations, and throughout society. It is indeed, as one of the chapters is titled, the church's moment.

STEVEN TIMMERMANS | Executive Director, The Christian Reformed Church in North America

Seeking Refuge is a must-read introductory book for Christians to understand and respond to one of the most controversial topics of our day: the global refugee crisis. The book gives the reader a broad exploration of the issues without losing sight of the individual stories that bring the crisis down to earth. If you want to know what it practically means to obey the command "love those who are foreigners," this is the book for you.

RICH NATHAN | Senior Pastor, Vineyard Columbus

Seeking Refuge is the best work to date when it comes to understanding present realities, global challenges, and practical responses to refugees in light of our kingdom citizenship. Filled with numerous stories and easy-to-understand explanations of technical matters, Bauman, Soerens, and Smeir have provided the church with a call to action and excellent assistance along the way. If you are looking for a one-stop shop to be informed, challenged, and led, then you have found it here!

J. D. PAYNE | Pastor, missiologist, and author, *Strangers Next Door: Immigration, Migration and Mission*

This highly readable and informative volume is the resource for God's people who hear about the global refugee crisis, have some questions, and don't know what to do. Inspiring and clarifying, groups in local congregations and groups of Christian citizens can apply the authors' practical and faithful recommendations immediately. I am profoundly thankful to God for inspiring such a biblically-based and moving book.

STEPHANIE SUMMERS | CEO, Center for Public Justice

This is an excellent primer for people of faith! A true North Star for understanding the faith perspective on immigration. A must read for believers!

DR. GUS REYES | Director, Christian Life Commission, Texas Baptists

Those who seek straight answers to hard questions will find them here amid the oft-confusing and ill-informed public rhetoric. Those who seek stories of real refugee struggles will get a very personal introduction here from Stephan, Matthew, and Issam, who have stared into these faces, becoming, like our Lord, men of sorrows, acquainted with grief (Isa. 53:3). *Seeking Refuge* doesn't turn 60 million people into mere facts, nor have they oversimplified their faces into a single story.

DAVID DRURY | Chief of Staff, The Wesleyan Church World Headquarters, founder of Immigrant Connection, and author of nine books including *Transforming Presence*

SEEKING REFUGE

ON THE SHORES OF THE GLOBAL REFUGEE CRISIS

STEPHAN BAUMAN, MATTHEW SOERENS, AND DR. ISSAM SMEIR

Moody Publishers

CHICAGO

Published in association with the literary agency of D. C. JACOBSON & ASSOCIATES, LLC, an author management company, www.dcjacobson.com

All Scripture quotations, unless otherwise indicated, are taken from the Holy Bible, New International Version®, NIV®. Copyright © 1973, 1978, 1984, 2011 by Biblica, Inc.™ Used by permission of Zondervan. All rights reserved worldwide. www.zondervan.com. The "NIV" and "New International Version" are trademarks registered in the United States Patent and Trademark Office by Biblica, Inc.™

Scripture quotations marked ESV are taken from *The Holy Bible, English Standard Version.* Copyright © 2000, 2001 by Crossway Bibles, a division of Good News Publishers. Used by permission. All rights reserved.

Scripture quotations marked NLT are taken from the *Holy Bible, New Living Translation,* copyright © 1996, 2004, 2007, 2013, 2015. Used by permission of Tyndale House Publishers, Inc., Wheaton, Illinois 60189, U.S.A. All rights reserved.

Edited by Ginger Kolbaba
Interior and Cover design: Erik M. Peterson
Cover photo of raft at sea copyright ©2014 by Paolo Cipriani/iStock (37074252). All rights reserved.

All websites and phone numbers listed herein are accurate at the time of publication but may change in the future or cease to exist. The listing of website references and resources does not imply publisher endorsement of the site's entire contents. Groups and organizations are listed for informational purposes, and listing does not imply publisher endorsement of their activities.

Some names within the text have been changed to protect the individuals' or their loved ones' privacy.

Library of Congress Cataloging-in-Publication Data

Names: Bauman, Stephan, author.
Title: Seeking refuge : on the shores of the global refugee crisis / Stephan Bauman, Matthew Soerens, and Dr. Issam Smeir.
Description: Chicago : Moody Publishers, 2016. | Includes bibliographical references.
Identifiers: LCCN 2016011767 | ISBN 9780802414885
Subjects: LCSH: Church work with refugees. | Refugees. | Asylum, Right of--Religious aspects--Christianity.
Classification: LCC BV4466 .B48 2016 | DDC 261.8/328--dc23 LC record available at http://lccn.loc.gov/2016011767

We hope you enjoy this book from Moody Publishers. Our goal is to provide high-quality, thought-provoking books and products that connect truth to your real needs and challenges. For more information on other books and products written and produced from a biblical perspective, go to www.moodypublishers.com or write to:

Moody Publishers
820 N. LaSalle Boulevard
Chicago, IL 60610

3 5 7 9 10 8 6 4 2

Printed in the United States of America

For our children—Joshua and Caleb; Zipporah and Zephaniah; Laith, Liam, Luke, and Zain—and for ten million refugee children throughout the world, with the prayer that you might each have the opportunity to flourish.

CONTENTS

FOREWORD

Several months ago in Iraq I (Lynne) met with a woman recently rescued from ISIS. Part of a small religious minority viciously targeted by ISIS, she was one of thousands of women who had been kidnapped and held as sex slaves for over a year. Many remain enslaved, but those who have been rescued are now cared for by local Iraqis with help from American Christians. In addition to trauma counseling, the women and their families are receiving food, shelter, medical care—and hope.

Though I'd previously traveled to other war zones, I'd never felt such a real and immediate danger, and I didn't make the trip to Iraq lightly. I went because I knew that for me, as a follower of Jesus, it was what love required. I'm not saying love always requires us to travel to war zones, or that it will be required of me again. But Jesus' way of love always asks something of us—some kind of risk.

For some of us it may be the risk of giving more generously than feels comfortable to organizations caring for refugees in the Middle East. I (Bill) recently visited churches and NGOs caring heroically for Syrian refugees in Jordan, providing refugees with short-term emergency relief like food, shelter, and medical relief, as well as longer-term interventions like educational opportunities and micro-enterprise. I was in awe of the way local Middle Eastern Christians embraced Muslim refugees with a spirit of respect, service, and love. And I was moved by the heartfelt gratitude of the refugee moms and dads who clearly love their kids as much as Lynne and I love ours.

But here's the sad truth: every organization serving refugees in Jordan, Lebanon, Turkey, Iraq, and even inside Syria is underfunded and overwhelmed. This is the greatest humanitarian crisis in the world—millions of victims of war continue to flee for their very lives—but all too often they escape the violence of bombs only to face the violence of hunger and illness and homelessness. At a large pastor's gathering just weeks ago I challenged every single pastor to raise as much money as possible for the organizations and churches that are being the hands and feet of Jesus in the midst of this crisis. Middle Eastern heroes like the ones I met need some heroically generous Americans to get behind them. We can do that!

For other Christians, love requires not just financial generosity, but a generosity of spirit and hospitality. We recently received an email from a pastor's wife in Germany. "At Christmas," she wrote, "my husband and I welcomed 150 refugees who moved into a government-provided facility right next to our church. We invited local Germans to join us for a celebration with the refugees and so many people came it was standing room only. What a celebration! It felt like we were in the middle of Syria! In February, 150 new people will arrive and we might have to let some sleep in the church. What a privilege! I don't feel like we are in a crisis. God is giving us the chance to welcome people and it is blessing our church with a new spirit!"

We pray that spirit will characterize every American church—and churches everywhere—as we warmly welcome refugees into our communities!

Some people—including some Christians—have allowed fear to dominate the refugee conversation. This book thoughtfully counters the falsehoods that give rise to much of that fear, and calls each of us to be bold agents of Jesus' transforming love. The violence of war and hatred is unmaking the world. We believe the only power strong enough to stand against that evil and remake the world is the power of God's love lived out by God's people. May we—God's church—answer that call.

BILL & LYNNE HYBELS
Senior Pastor and Advocate for Global Engagement, Willow Creek Community Church

CHAPTER 1

AN UNPRECEDENTED GLOBAL CRISIS

Today, an estimated sixty million people worldwide have been forcibly displaced from their homes, a number larger than at any time in recorded history.[1] While many remain within the borders of their country, about twenty million individuals have been forced by persecution to escape, seeking refuge in a neighboring land. More than half of those refugees are children.[2]

Our minds can only scarcely comprehend these statistics. Individual stories and images are what have ignited unprecedented global attention to the plight of refugees. In September 2015, nearly five years into a deadly civil war, the world's attention dramatically focused upon the conflict in Syria and the displacement it has engendered. With one photograph that hit newspapers and social media, millions witnessed the lifeless body of a three-year-old boy, Alan Kurdi, washed up on a Turkish beach after a failed attempt to reach safety in Europe. Filmmaker Ken Burns, reflecting on that photograph, observed: "The power of the single image to convey complex information is still there. It has that power to shock and arrest us. To make us stop for just a second and interrupt the flow."[3]

Wincing as we glanced at the little boy, still wearing tiny shoes and a red T-shirt, we could not help but think of our own children. We grieve the loss of innocent life. We shudder to imagine the horror that would inspire a parent to embark upon such a dangerous journey, and, in a subconscious pivot from compassion to fear, wonder if such terror could reach our shores—our children—as well. We ask God why He allows such horrific injustice and suffering. And in response, we might hear the still, small voice of God asking His church, *How will you respond?*

In recent years, about 105,000 refugees have been resettled annually to developed countries. Nearly one million more have made their way to Europe to seek asylum. Yet these numbers account for only a small fraction of the world's displaced people.

This book is designed to be a tool for the church—followers of Jesus in every part of the world—to answer that question in ways informed both by the Bible and by the facts of the current crisis. While we hope what's written here will be useful to those of any faith or of no faith, our focus is particularly informed by our shared Christian worldview and by our conviction that, to quote pastor Bill Hybels, "The local church is the hope of the world."[4] We believe that the church, in its many local incarnations throughout the world, must be at the center of the response to the global refugee crisis. That includes those, like the three of us, who form the church in the West: as columnist Michael Gerson, writing from Lebanon, a nation where nearly one in four residents is now a refugee, observes, "If American churches . . . are not relevant here, they are irrelevant."[5]

As American citizens (two of us by birth, one by naturalization), our focus in *Seeking Refuge* is primarily on how local churches and individual Christ followers in the West—in the United States, in particular, but also in Canada, Europe, and beyond—might best respond to the refugee crisis. In recent years, about 105,000 refugees (from all countries, not just Syria) have been resettled annually to developed countries, including around 70,000 that the United States accepted in 2015. Nearly one million more have made their own way to Europe in 2015 to seek asylum.[6] Yet these numbers account for only a small fraction of the world's displaced people.[7] The vast majority of refugees live *outside* of the West, generally in developing countries adjacent to the homelands they have been forced to flee. Most of those people find shelter in refugee camps or urban settings where basic needs such as food and water are often in short supply, and where most are barred from working to support themselves. As Christians in the West, our primary focus must be to support our brothers and sisters in these countries bearing the most significant weight of the refugee crisis.

Nevertheless, while the number of refugees who arrive on the shores of the Chesapeake Bay or Lake Michigan (near to our respective homes) or elsewhere in North America account for just a small fraction of all displaced people globally, they present the most proximate opportunity to respond with compassion. We need not and ought not choose between caring for refugees locally and caring for refugees overseas, because how we respond *here* directly impacts what happens *there*. The world is watching how we in the United States respond to the relatively few refugees who reach our shores, and our government's encouragement to other nations to protect those fleeing persecution lacks credibility if we do not do our part.

As Christians, our faith compels us to respond with welcome even as we support those helping the much larger numbers of displaced people elsewhere in the world. Reacting to this crisis will require much more from the Western church than simply sending a check overseas: while we can and should help financially, we must also emulate our brothers and sisters throughout the world who are responding with generous hospitality.

It is also important to note that, while much of the recent media coverage on refugees has been focused on the shores of the Mediterranean—on the refugee crisis emanating from Syria's civil war in particular, which has driven hundreds of thousands to seek safety in Europe and ignited fiery debates over whether Syrian refugees should be welcomed into the United States—this refugee crisis is much broader. This crisis is indeed global, affecting people on the shores of Africa's Lake Kivu and Lake Tanganyika, of the Andaman and South China Seas in Southeast Asia, and of the Pacific Ocean in Central America, among others.

Major Source Countries of Refugees

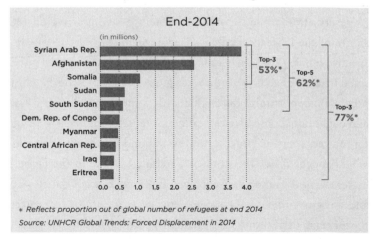

* Reflects proportion out of global number of refugees at end 2014
Source: UNHCR Global Trends: Forced Displacement in 2014

Until recently, the response of most Westerners to refugees was generally one of sympathy. The US refugee resettlement program, though perhaps not widely understood, enjoyed bipartisan support in Congress and drew criticism only from a small segment of Americans. While broader immigration issues, including border security and how to respond to those in the country unlawfully, have long been controversial, refugees—who all enter the United States with full legal status, and who, by definition, have fled persecution and thus almost always have compelling stories—have not been particularly controversial.[8]

By late 2015, however, the question of refugee resettlement had become contentious, particularly as the refugee crisis fueled by the Syrian conflict and the arrival of hundreds of thousands of asylum seekers into Europe dominated news headlines. Anti-refugee sentiment further intensified after the horrific terrorist attacks in Paris and then in California, which led many to speculate that the US refugee resettlement program could be infiltrated by terrorists. The US House of Representatives, where refugee resettlement had long enjoyed broad bipartisan support, voted in November 2015 to dramatically halt resettlement of refugees from Syria and Iraq, while another bill proposed a moratorium on refugee resettlement altogether. Governors of more than thirty states announced their opposition to Syrian refugees being resettled within their states. A Bloomberg News poll found that a slim majority of Americans (53 percent) now wanted the United States to abandon an announced plan to resettle ten thousand Syrian refugees in the upcoming year.[9]

The question of refugees—and refugee resettlement, in particular—has divided the church as well. Many Christians feel torn between the natural desire to protect themselves and their families and the desire to minister compassionately to the vulnerable. Given the scope of this crisis, how Christ followers respond to this tension could define the church for a generation or more.

OUR PERSPECTIVE

Our perspective on the refugee crisis is closely informed by our many years of experience in serving and resettling refugees in partnership with local churches through World Relief, the organization we serve. World Relief was formed in 1944, in response to the devastation and displacement of millions of refugees caused by World War II. The people of Park Street Church in Boston resolved to forego meals and send the money they would have spent on food to what they called the "War Relief Fund." When other churches, linked through the National Association of Evangelicals, joined the effort, they collectively raised $600,000—in today's dollars, nearly $8 million—to help rebuild Europe. Over time, as that sacrificial compassion extended to serve other regions plagued by poverty and conflict, the War Relief Fund became World Relief.

Since the late 1970s, World Relief has been one of fewer than a dozen national agencies—and the only distinctly evangelical organization—authorized by the US State Department to resettle refugees within the United States. Our resettlement program began when a couple named Grady and Evelyn Mangham, who had served for many years as missionaries in Vietnam with The Christian and Missionary Alliance, wanted to help churches in the United States welcome Vietnamese refugees. The Manghams worked with the US State Department, as well as their denomination and World Relief, to find local churches throughout the country to welcome refugees. From those origins, World Relief has helped to welcome more than 275,000 refugees into our nation, partnering alongside thousands of local churches and tens of thousands of church-based volunteers.

While we are committed to presenting fairly the diverging views on this complex and now controversial topic, we do not come to the question of how to respond to refugees as dispassionate observers: in our work with World Relief, each of us, from different vantage points, has been a practitioner deeply involved in serving refugees, driven by our belief that doing so is an important way that we can live out Jesus' command to love our neighbors (Matt. 22:39). Though we each work toward the same mission of empowering local churches to serve the vulnerable, we bring different experiences and perspectives to this topic.

Stephan's Story

In our early twenties, my wife, Belinda, and I left our rural hometown in Wisconsin for what was meant to be a six-month stint in West Africa, working with Mercy Ships. I took a leave of absence from my career in business and Belinda from hers as a schoolteacher. Having barely traveled, we were inexperienced and naïve. Within months the directors asked us to colead a medical team among two warring tribes in Northern Ghana. It was here, in the bush, where we first experienced how violence devastates people, often destroying their homes and tearing families apart.

It was several years later, though, while working in the Balkans near the end of the Bosnian war, that I began to seriously grapple with forced migration. I met refugees in the process of fleeing—Bosnians, mainly, but also Croatians and Serbians—who were forced to escape their homes because of the conflict. Some were nearly killed; many had lost family members. All wished they could return home. But they couldn't.

One man had fled his home in Bosnia with his wife and his accordion. Although he had lost everything else, including family members, he remained hopeful that someday he could rebuild his life. His accordion became his means to earn a living.

Today, two decades later, I serve as president of World Relief.

Helping refugees, both internationally and domestically, is a major area of focus for us. It's an honor to work alongside my colleagues on the front lines in the United States and in countries where people are displaced, such as Jordan, Iraq, Turkey, South Sudan, Congo, and many others.

I recently returned from Jordan where I met a pastor who opened his church to Syrian refugee children and their mothers to learn life skills and participate in activities to overcome their trauma. When he did, however, many people from his congregation left for good. Even kids from the community taunted Syrian children as they walked to the church.

"They come to us bleeding," he said. But he told me how his church has changed for the better. "For so many years we tried to share God's love to the people in Syria but we were stopped. Now Syria has come to us and to our church." It is a privilege to work with churches like this one and others throughout the globe who are responding to the crisis in profound ways.

Issam's Story

I was born in Mafraq, Jordan, a city that is known today for hosting the largest Syrian refugee camp in the world. At that time, however, Mafraq was a small Bedouin town on the edge of the desert that hardly anyone had heard of.

While growing up in Jordan, I became accustomed to wars, crises, and refugees. Over the years Jordan became an oasis of peace in a troubled region, hosting millions of refugees (Palestinians, Lebanese, Iraqis, Libyans, and finally Syrians). When I was seven years old, our local church welcomed several Lebanese families who had fled civil war in their country. At that time, the idea of refugees did not mean much to me. The children whom I befriended from Lebanon were just like other friends who came to live in our town and attended school with us. They moved with their families after a year or two, to settle in a faraway country called the USA. I never heard from my friends again, but often wondered what had become of them.

My first encounter with the word *refugee* was quite personal. One day as a child I opened the door to an old woman whom I did not recognize. The woman was wearing a colorful dress and carried many bags. She knew my name, so I ran deeper into the house to call my mom. My mom was very excited: this old woman was my grand-mother. She had come to visit us from the West Bank/Palestine. I later learned that my parents had left their small town of Nisf Ju-beil in the West Bank and moved to live in Jordan after the second Arab-Israeli war. They could not go back. That day *refugee* became personal. I was a refugee's son.

Twenty-five years after that incident, in 2000, I came to the Unit-ed States to study clinical psychology at Wheaton College. The peace process between the Israelis and Palestinians had just collapsed. The news from the region was bad. I recalled spending most of my day reading and listening to disturbing reports that left me angry and resentful. During that time one of my professors asked another in-ternational student, who I discovered later was an Israeli, to open the class with a prayer for peace in the Middle East.

A few days later, the Israeli student approached me and invited me to his house for dinner. I was surprised by his invitation, but more stunned that I accepted. I walked to his house that evening with many questions ruminating in my mind. What if we ended up argu-ing about politics? What if he was rude or insensitive to me?

Fortunately, none of that happened, and the evening turned out to be pleasant. While playing with his children after dinner, for the first time it hit me that this man was just like me. We were experiencing opportunities that our fathers never had. We were both told things about each other that were not true.

Over the years our friendship deepened. Whenever I heard news that made me angry and resentful, I remembered my friend and his family. I needed him, as much as he needed me, to give me the right perspective, that we are all created in God's image. Today as I look back at that encounter, I have come to believe that God was preparing me for the next chapter of my life. I needed to find inner peace before I could help others find it.

As I was finishing my studies in the United States, I received a call from the director of the counseling center at a World Relief office, asking me to help a newly resettled Iraqi refugee who was struggling to adjust to his new life in this country. The refugee was a military officer in the Iraqi army. He was having such a difficult time adjusting to his new entry-level job that he had threatened to go on a hunger strike until World Relief would find him different work. Later I joined World Relief as a full-time counselor, and for the last fifteen years, I have counseled traumatized refugees who are dealing with a haunting past and a challenging present.

If I had one word with which to summarize my work with refugees, it would be *stories*. Most whom I have spent time with have had one thing in common: a horrific story of trauma and loss. Day in and day out, young moms have shared with me about being forced to abandon their babies. Men have told me about being raped repeatedly in prison, and boys have recalled walking for months in jungles, seeking safety and witnessing friends eaten alive by wild animals.

Stories of triumph against all odds are common as well. I always enjoy working with new groups of people. The Somali Bantu population, an ethnic group systematically enslaved for decades in Africa, was particularly interesting. They came to the United States after living for many years in tents in Kenya. When they arrived in this country, they had to catch up on hundreds of years of technology. I witnessed Somali Bantu children on their first day in the United States stand in the shower and squeal with delight at the sight of water sprinkles, which they had never seen before. Today some of those children are in college.

Between the tears, I have also heard many funny stories of cultural misunderstandings that, though perhaps frustrating at the time, we could eventually all laugh at. Once, a refugee who was not aware of the "daylight savings time" concept went to work one hour early for several days before finally understanding the time change. It actually ended up helping him with his reputation for tardiness at work!

While I continued to serve refugees resettled to suburban Chicago, in 2011, I also began to spend three months each year in countries such as Libya, Tunisia, Egypt, Jordan, Turkey, and Lebanon. As one of a few Arabic-speaking experts in trauma therapy, I train local mental health professionals and supervise their work from a distance via the Internet. While this experience has been extremely rewarding, it has not involved the local church in these afflicted nations. I have prayed for an opportunity to help the church shine as a city on a hill, serving as an oasis for healing.

In 2015, my prayers were answered when a local Syrian church leader, whom I had never met, called and asked me to train Syrian Christian leaders in the area of trauma therapy. Two months later, I spent four days with fifteen Syrian church leaders—Jesuit priests, nuns, doctors, and others from the provinces of Aleppo, Homs, and Damascus—at a monastery in Lebanon. Every morning, I awoke to the sound of hymns, eager to meet with these brothers and sisters who were filled with a joy and peace that "transcends all understanding" (Phil. 4:7).

In the last day of training, I noticed a shift in the mood among the group. The road between Damascus and Beirut had been captured by rebel groups, which meant that the nine church leaders from Aleppo would not be able to go home, I had to leave the next day. On my way back to the States, I remembered God's promise to those among us who have suffered most: "He will wipe every tear from their eyes. There will be no more death or mourning or crying or pain, for the old order of things has passed away" (Rev. 21:4). It is that promise that I hold dear to my heart. I pray that you and I will be part of God's work as we yearn for that day when He makes all things right.

Matthew's Story

Quite in contrast to Issam, for most of my life, I had little to no awareness of immigration issues. I grew up in a small city in northeastern Wisconsin where, though a small Hmong population lived nearby, I do not ever recall personally interacting with a refugee.

My first exposure to these issues came as a senior at Wheaton College in suburban Chicago. A friend, Anna Ruth, had signed up to volunteer with the local World Relief office and had been paired with a family of seven from Rwanda. Anna Ruth had spent a lot of time with the four daughters in this family, but she thought that their adolescent son, Denis, would benefit from a male mentor, so she invited me to come with her.

Denis and his family quickly became my close friends. When I graduated from college, I rented an apartment in their apartment complex, a remarkably vibrant neighborhood where World Relief had resettled refugees from more than a dozen countries. I lived there for about eight years and, in that time, many of my refugee and other immigrant neighbors became my close friends.

I also began working for World Relief's local Immigrant Legal Services program, where a major component of my job was to help refugees apply for their green cards (one year after their arrival, per US law) and then for citizenship (five years after arrival). Becoming acquainted with US immigration law gave me a much deeper understanding of the barriers refugees must overcome to make it to the United States, and of the need for governmental policy changes.

For the past several years, the focus of my work with World Relief has been to equip local churches throughout the country to think about refugees and other immigrants from a distinctly biblical perspective and then to apply the teachings of Scripture to welcome and serve these vulnerable populations. Much of my work has focused on the long-controversial question of how both the church and our government ought to respond to the complex question of immigrants who are present unlawfully in the United States. By contrast, refugees, who enter the States with full legal status, have always been relatively uncontroversial. In the past year, though, that has changed, with refugee resettlement becoming a politically charged issue. More than ever, my passion is to see the church respond well, in biblically informed, missionally minded ways, to these complex issues.

THE ROAD AHEAD

Our personal experiences have convinced us that Christ followers ought to be at the center of the global refugee crisis solution—which is where we hope your story intersects with ours. In the chapters that follow, we have sought to provide a biblically grounded perspective and orientation to the topic of refugees. As we consider what the Bible has to say about these displaced people, we become better able to engage this complex issue. With that foundation, we will unpack who these vulnerable individuals are and how refugee resettlement works, addressing many of the most common concerns and, by conveying stories, seek to put human faces on these displaced people so often described merely as statistics. We will also explore the situations that refugees are fleeing, provide practical guidance on how to minister to them effectively, and explore the policy issues that impact their lives and well-being. Finally, we will cast a vision for how local churches might respond, applying our faith to one of the most urgent yet complicated issues of our time.

Our core conviction is that the church is God's solution to this unprecedented global crisis, and it requires us to rise up to respond in mission-driven, fact-based ways to this tremendous crisis. While we would not attempt to explain why God has allowed the persecution and violence that has compelled so many people to flee, we believe that He has purposes even in the midst of horrendous suffering, and that He is already working to build His church and expand His kingdom through the global refugee crisis. We hope and pray that you will join in what God is doing in the midst of this unique time in history.

CHAPTER 2

JESUS WAS A REFUGEE:

THINKING BIBLICALLY ABOUT MIGRATION

For those who profess to follow Jesus, our top authority on any topic—but particularly on a complex one—ought to be the Bible. For many evangelical Christians, though, refugees and immigration are thought of as political, economic, and cultural issues, rather than as a biblical concern. A recent LifeWay Research survey of American evangelical Christians found that just 12 percent said that they think about immigration issues primarily from the perspective of the Bible.[1] In fact, when asked what most influenced their thinking on this topic, the Bible, the local church, and national Christian leaders *combined* were reported less often than the media.

The problem is not merely that many Christians are paying more attention to the television, radio, and Facebook status updates than they are to their pastors—it's also that relatively few of those who *are* in church on a regular basis have ever been encouraged to think about the plight of refugees from a biblical perspective. Only about one in five evangelical Christians report that they have ever been challenged by their local church to reach out to refugees or other immigrants in their community.[2]

Obviously some contemporary social or political issues are not typically discussed in a church context since they are not addressed directly in Scripture. For example, while we can certainly apply biblical principles in one direction or another, debates over marginal income tax rates or the appropriateness of gun control are not mentioned directly in the Bible, so at best we can make prudential judgments informed by biblical values.

But as we examine the question of how to treat refugees and other immigrants, the Bible actually has *a lot* to say. The Hebrew word *ger*—translated variously into English as *foreigner*, *resident alien*, *stranger*, *sojourner*, or *immigrant*—appears ninety-two times in the Old Testament.[3] Many of those references mention God's particular concern for the foreigner alongside two other vulnerable groups: orphans and widows. Scholar Walter Kaiser notes that the Old Testament warns "no fewer than thirty-six times of Israel's obligations to aliens, widows, and orphans. Most important here, Israel's obligation is to be motivated by the memory that they had been aliens in Egypt."[4] By the count of theologian Orlando Espín, "Welcoming the stranger . . . is the most often repeated commandment in the Hebrew Scriptures, with the exception of the imperative to worship only the one God."[5]

For whatever reason, though, we do not often discuss God's commandments to love and welcome foreigners in our local churches, which is likely why only about half of American evangelicals say that they are very familiar with what the Bible says about how immigrants should be treated.[6]

The question of how we respond to refugees is not *only* a biblical question—there are valid and important questions of foreign policy, economics, security, and cultural cohesion that we can and, in subsequent chapters, will address. But for those of us who profess that the Scriptures are authoritative, that is where we ought to begin the conversation about how we interact with those who come as foreigners into our country and our communities.

JESUS WAS A REFUGEE . . . AND SO WERE MANY OTHER BIBLICAL HEROES

In December 2015, as Canada was receiving the first of twenty-five thousand Syrian refugees that the country resettled over the course of three months, an Anglican church in Newfoundland posted this sign: "Christmas: A Story about a Middle East Family Seeking Refuge."[7]

The account of Christ's incarnation is certainly about much more than *just* a family's flight as refugees, of course, but that our Lord and Savior, as He took on human flesh, stepped personally into the refugee experience is not inconsequential. Our nativity scenes and Christmas pageants usually include the gift-bearing magi, but often stop the story there, just before Jesus, Mary, and Joseph were forced as refugees to flee a tyrannical government:

> *When [the magi] had gone, an angel of the Lord appeared to Joseph in a dream. "Get up," he said, "take the child and his mother and escape to Egypt. Stay there until I tell you, for Herod is going to search for the child to kill him."*
>
> *So he got up, took the child and his mother during the night and left for Egypt, where he stayed until the death of Herod.* (Matt. 2:13–15)

The biblical text provides very few details about either the journey to Egypt—which, from Bethlehem to the border with Egypt at that time, outside of Herod's dominion, would have been several days' journey—or about how Jesus, Mary, and Joseph were treated once they arrived. If human history is any indicator, though, it is likely that some would have responded with compassion and hospitality, and likely others would have treated them as a nuisance or even a threat. We can only speculate: Were they able to find shelter? Were they welcomed or harassed?[8] Did local carpenters gripe that Joseph was driving down their wages? Was Jesus suspected of carrying a disease?

One thing is clear: the millions of refugees in our world today have an advocate in Jesus, who was "made like them, fully human in every way" (Heb. 2:17), able "to empathize with our weaknesses" (4:15)—even with the particular experience of having to flee one's home in the middle of the night in search of refuge. "The importance of the depiction of Jesus and his family as refugees should not be underestimated," writes theologian Fleur Houston. "Jesus can empathize with refugees in their sufferings, enables endurance, and brings hope."[9]

While certainly the most important refugee in the biblical narrative, Jesus is not the only biblical figure to have been forcibly displaced. Jacob fled his homeland under the threat of violence from his brother, Esau (Gen. 27:42–44). Moses fled from Egypt to Midian, initially, because Pharaoh sought to kill him (Ex. 2:15). When being persecuted unjustly by King Saul, David escaped on multiple occasions to the land of the Philistines, where he sought asylum under King Achish (1 Sam. 21:10; 27:1). Similarly, the prophet Elijah evaded the persecution of the evil King Ahab and Queen Jezebel by traveling out into the wilderness; so desperate was his situation that he "prayed that he might die" (1 Kings 19:1–4). In the New Testament, we see how persecution in Jerusalem forced the earliest followers of Jesus to scatter—and also how God ultimately used this evil for good, as these apostles took the gospel with them and planted some of the earliest churches (Acts 8:1, 4–5). Then, as now, God can work through even the most brutal and unjust situations to advance His purposes.

THE GREAT COMMANDMENT:
"GO AND DO LIKEWISE . . ."

Jesus not only *was* a refugee; He also taught His disciples in many ways that inform how *we* can respond to refugees.

In a commandment that Jesus said summed up the entirety of the Law and the Prophets, Jesus told His disciples to "do to others what you would have them do to you" (Matt. 7:12). Our local World Relief offices in the United States offer refugee simulations to help people experience in a small way the difficult decisions refugees face. Suppose, for example, that at some distant point in the future it became unsafe to be a Christian in your country. After your pastor has been arrested, rumors circulate that government agents will be at your house soon, ready to torture, rape, or kill you. You have no choice but to gather a few vital possessions and leave in the middle of the night. What would you take with you? Where would you go? And most important, how would you hope to be treated once you arrived? The Golden Rule guides us to use that question as the standard for how we should treat those who come as refugees to our land.

Another of Jesus' teachings that the Bible describes as encompassing the entirety of the law (Gal. 5:14) is the second half of the Great Commandment. Questioned by a legal scholar, Jesus affirmed that the most important commandments, essential to inheriting eternal life, are, "'Love the Lord your God with all your heart and with all your soul and with all your strength and with all your mind'; and,

'Love your neighbor as yourself'" (Luke 10:27).

We suspect that, if He had left it there, most of us would be inclined to define "neighbor" as narrowly as possible, to limit our own responsibilities. But the lawyer in the story asked a clarifying question: "Who is my neighbor?" Jesus' response makes clear that our "neighbor" includes anyone who is in need, not just those who share our ethnicity, our religion, or our zip code.

To make His point, Jesus told the story of a man who was beaten and left alongside the road to Jericho. The religious leaders of his day, a priest and a Levite, walked by on the other side of the road. They were important people and likely had important places to be. They may also have been thinking of their *own* safety. But a Samaritan saw the beaten man, stopped what he was doing, recognized his humanity, and, moved with compassion, treated his wounds and took him to an inn where he could recover.

That Jesus made a Samaritan the hero of this story is notable. Samaritans were not "good" in the minds of the average Jewish listener: they were considered foreigners (Luke 17:18) and were viewed as heretics for their theological beliefs, which Jesus elsewhere acknowledged as errant (John 4:22). So despised were the Samaritans that a couple of Jesus' disciples proposed that Jesus destroy one of their villages with fire, but He rebuked that suggestion (Luke 9:51–55). Indeed, Jesus' approach to these marginalized foreigners was entirely countercultural: He "had to go through Samaria" (John 4:4), even though there were other, less direct routes that some Jews may have preferred in order to avoid contact with Samaritans.[10] When He did, He interacted compassionately with a Samaritan woman, revealing Himself to her as the Messiah and equipping her to be among the first evangelists (John 4:4–42). Elsewhere, Jesus praised a Samaritan as a model of gratitude (Luke 17:11–19). And here, in response to a lawyer's efforts "to justify himself" (Luke 10:29), Jesus offered a Samaritan as the model of neighborly love who extended compassion for a stranger in need—and told us to "go and do likewise" (Luke 10:37).

If this legal scholar knew the law well, he would have realized that God's original command to the Israelites to love their neighbors, recorded for us in Leviticus 19:18, was followed almost immediately by a specific command to love the foreigner, as if anticipating the human inclination to narrowly limit our neighborly responsibilities to those who share our nationality: "When a foreigner resides among you in your land, do not mistreat them. The foreigner residing among you must be treated as your native-born. Love them as yourself, for you were foreigners in Egypt. I am the LORD your God" (Lev. 19:33–34).

Notably, the Samaritan probably could tell very little about the man beaten along the side of the road: he was stripped of his clothes, which might have provided some indication of his social status or ethnic group, and he likely could not speak, so there was no accent to give away his origins. The Samaritan could not have known any of these details, and he did not need to: he merely needed to observe that the man needed help.

The application to the current refugee crisis is clear: by Jesus' standard, the refugee—whether from Syria, Somalia, or Burma, whether living one mile or ten thousand miles from us, whether Christian, Muslim, Buddhist, or an atheist, and whatever else might distinguish them—is our neighbor. The command of Jesus is to love them. That there may be risk or cost involved is not relevant to the mandate to love.[11]

FEARFULLY AND WONDERFULLY MADE

We ought to love refugees because they are our neighbors, but also because the Bible teaches us to value them since, like us, they are made in the image of God. Old Testament scholar Daniel Carroll argues that, as we apply Scripture to our thinking about immigration, we should start "in the beginning," in the book of Genesis.[12] Even before we encounter any specific biblical injunctions of how to treat the refugee or other foreigners, we find that each human being—refugees certainly included—is made by God and in His image (Gen. 1:27).

Each human being, regardless of ethnicity, gender, legal status, disability, or any other qualifier, is "fearfully and wonderfully made" by the creator God (Ps. 139:14), and as such has inherent dignity. We value and protect human life because we believe it is precious to God. That commitment to life compels us to do all we can to shelter and protect refugees, who in many cases have been forced to flee to preserve their lives.

The sacredness of human life is amplified by the incarnation: that Jesus Christ, the Son of God, became fully human. Russell Moore, president of the Southern Baptist Convention's Ethics and Religious Liberty Commission, observes, "Jesus identified himself with humanity—in all of our weakness and fragility."[13] He adds:

> If Jesus shares humanity with us, and if the goal of the kingdom is humanity in Christ, then life must matter to the church. The church must proclaim in its teaching and embody in its practices love and justice for those the outside world would wish to silence or kill. And the mission of the church must be to proclaim everlasting life, and to work to honor every life made in the image of God, whether inside or outside of the people of God.[14]

That each person is made in the likeness of the creator God also suggests that, beyond inherent dignity, human beings have remarkable creative potential. Some of those most opposed to admitting more refugees or other immigrants into a given country are, fundamentally, concerned about more *people*, whom they see as a potential drain on limited resources, based on a repeatedly disproven Malthusian philosophy, which presumes that more people necessarily means *less* for the rest of us.[15] Groups opposed to refugee resettlement add up all the *costs* associated with refugees or other migrants as evidence of why they (or most of them, at least) should be kept out; but the economists who actually study migration issues, who perform not *cost analyses* but cost-*benefit* analyses, consistently find that immigrants actually contribute more, overall, to the economy of the receiving country than they receive from it.[16] That is because, as columnist Michael Gerson notes, "human beings are not just mouths but hands and brains."[17] Refugees do not merely consume; they are not mere "takers." As resilient and entrepreneurial people made in the image of their Creator, they also have remarkable capacity to produce, and we deny the image of God within them when we speak of refugees (or anyone) as a burden.

STANDING WITH THE PERSECUTED CHURCH

Refugees are our neighbors and have inherent human dignity regardless of their religious background. As Christians, we also have a particular concern for the many refugees who are our brothers and sisters in Christ persecuted for their faith. The apostle Paul wrote to the church in Galatia that we should "do good to all people, especially to those who belong to the family of believers" (Gal. 6:10). The church is composed of many distinct but interdependent members, he said, just like a human body, and "if one part suffers, every part

> Of approximately 125,000 Iraqi refugees admitted since 2007, more than 35 percent have been Christians— many times more than the Christian share of the Iraqi population— because Christians have been uniquely persecuted.

suffers with it" (1 Cor. 12:26).

The horrific reality is that many of our brothers and sisters around the globe today are suffering as they are persecuted for the name of Jesus. At the hands of governments hostile to the Christian faith and, increasingly, nonstate terrorists, Christ followers have been martyred. In fact, Open Doors USA's analysis suggests that 2015 may have been the most violent year for Christians in modern history.[18] In a single month, reports *Christianity Today,*

ISIS beheaded a Christian journalist in Syria. On the eastern edge of Africa, a group of Somali militants named al-Shabaab targeted Christians in an attack on a Kenyan college in April that killed as many as 150. The same month, ISIS executed dozens of Ethiopian Christians.[19]

Many believers have been given a stark non-option: flee, renounce your Christian faith, or die.[20] As ISIS (also known as ISIL or Daesh) targets ancient Christian communities in Iraq and Syria—a situation US Secretary of State John Kerry has characterized as genocide[21]—it has forced hundreds of thousands to flee their homes and, in many cases, their countries. Similarly, but largely out of the media spotlight, Baptist, Catholic, and Anglican Christ followers from among various ethnic minorities in Burma have, for many years, had to escape to Thailand, Malaysia, or India, where they live either in refugee camps or without legal protections in urban areas.[22] Hundreds of Christian children have been kidnapped, thousands of people killed, and thousands of others displaced from their homes by Boko Haram terrorists in Nigeria.[23]

To stand in solidarity with the persecuted church, we ought to do all we can to stop these horrific situations of persecution. Whenever possible, we should strive and pray for circumstances such that Christians would not be forced to leave. When they make the decision that fleeing is their only option, though, local churches in receiving countries also must do everything possible to welcome them.

We have many opportunities to support our persecuted brothers and sisters through the US refugee resettlement program as well: about 340,000 professing Christians of one tradition or another have been admitted into the United States as refugees between 2003 and 2015, more than of any other religious tradition.[24] Many of those individuals and families were persecuted particularly because of their Christian faith. Of approximately 125,000 Iraqi refugees admitted since 2007, for example, more than 35 percent have been Christians—many times more than the Christian share of the Iraqi population—because Christians have been uniquely persecuted.[25] Similarly, more than 100,000 persecuted Christians from Burma have been admitted to the United States as refugees in the past decade: though Christians make up less than 5 percent of the total population of Burma, they compose more than 70 percent of the refugees from that country.[26]

If we were forced to flee our country, we would hope that a Christian brother or sister in the country to which we fled would be there to welcome us, to help us adjust, and to lament with us what we had lost. We have the opportunity to stand with the persecuted church as many come into our country each year. At World Relief, our hope

Where Do Refugees Resettled by World Relief Come From?

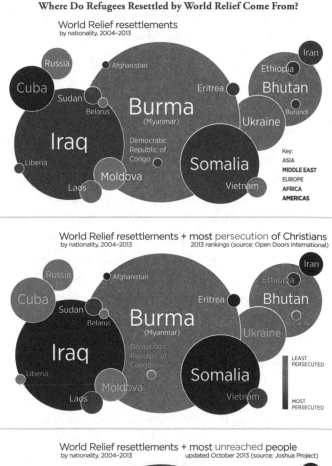

World Relief resettlements
by nationality, 2004–2013

Russia · Afghanistan · Cuba · Sudan · Belarus · Burma (Myanmar) · Eritrea · Iran · Ethiopia · Bhutan · Burundi · Ukraine · Iraq · Democratic Republic of Congo · Liberia · Somalia · Moldova · Laos · Vietnam

Key:
ASIA
MIDDLE EAST
EUROPE
AFRICA
AMERICAS

World Relief resettlements + most persecution of Christians
by nationality, 2004–2013   2013 rankings (source: Open Doors International)

LEAST PERSECUTED

MOST PERSECUTED

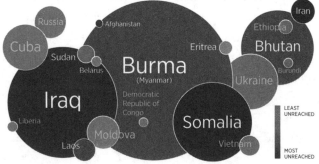

World Relief resettlements + most unreached people
by nationality, 2004–2013   updated October 2013 (source: Joshua Project)

LEAST UNREACHED

MOST UNREACHED

is to have a Good Neighbor Team from a local church at the airport to greet each refugee who arrives, who will then walk alongside them through the first several months of their adjustment, and who will hopefully build a friendship that lasts far beyond the initial resettlement period, right into eternity.

The church in the West—where few of us have ever faced any sort of real persecution—actually has a great deal to learn from our refugee brothers and sisters, many of whom have a deep, vibrant faith, refined by oppression. The body of Christ is composed of different but all vital parts: our persecuted brothers and sisters need our solidarity, advocacy, and (for those admitted as refugees to our home countries) welcome, but *we also need them*—they can teach us what it means to follow Jesus even when that decision is costly.

In the end, this is not just about standing with our brothers and sisters. It is about standing with Jesus Himself. Jesus takes personally the persecution of the church. When He confronted Saul on the road to Damascus, He asked him, who had zealously persecuted the early church, "Why do you persecute *me*?" (Acts 9:4, italics added). And He explained to His disciples that at the final judgment,

> *All the nations will be gathered before him, and he will separate the people one from another as a shepherd separates the sheep from the goats. He will put the sheep on his right and the goats on his left.*
>
> *Then the King will say to those on his right, "Come, you who are blessed by my Father; take your inheritance, the kingdom prepared for you since the creation of the world. For I was hungry and you gave me something to eat, I was thirsty and you gave me something to drink, I was a stranger and you invited me in, I needed clothes and you clothed me, I was sick and you*

looked after me, I was in prison and you came to visit me."

Then the righteous will answer him, "Lord, when did we see you hungry and feed you, or thirsty and give you something to drink? When did we see you a stranger and invite you in, or needing clothes and clothe you? When did we see you sick or in prison and go to visit you?"

The King will reply, "Truly I tell you, whatever you did for one of the least of these brothers and sisters of mine, you did for me." (Matt. 25:32–40)

When we welcome a stranger who is among "the least of these" brothers and sisters, we welcome Jesus Himself. If we fail to do so, Jesus continued in a sobering passage, we fail to welcome Him (Matt. 25:41–46).

THE GREAT COMMISSION: "GO AND MAKE DISCIPLES OF ALL NATIONS"

While we have a particular concern for persecuted Christians, our Christian faith compels us to be concerned with the plight of refugees of other faiths as well. Those who are not Christians are made in God's image, so their lives are precious, and they are our neighbors, whom we are called to love.

Shortly before ascending into heaven, Jesus left His disciples with this final charge: "Make disciples of all nations, baptizing them in the name of the Father and of the Son and of the Holy Spirit, and teaching them to obey everything I have commanded you" (Matt. 28:19–20). As recorded in the book of Acts, Jesus commanded His disciples to be His witnesses "in Jerusalem, and in all Judea and Samaria, and to the ends of the earth" (Acts 1:8). While the church can and must go "to the ends of the earth," we also can and must live out the Great Commission locally.[27] The reality that many refugees who arrive in our country are *not yet* Christ followers presents a remarkable opportunity to live out the Great Commission right within our communities.

That opportunity is not an accident: Scripture tells us that God "makes nations great, and destroys them; he enlarges nations, and disperses them" (Job 12:23), and Paul taught in Acts that God does this "so that [people] would seek him and perhaps reach out for him and find him" (Acts 17:27). God has a sovereign purpose in the migration of people, and He invites His church—here in the United States and throughout the world—to join Him in that work.

Just as was the case with the scattering of the apostles in the early church and has been true throughout church history, God uses migration as a tool to advance His purposes. As described by missiologist Enoch Wan, "diaspora mission"—the redemptive work of God through the migration of people—occurs in at least three ways:[28]

> More unreached people groups live *within the boundaries of the United States*—361—than in any other country besides India and China.

(1) Mission *to* the diaspora: Christ followers in the host country share the hope of the gospel with refugees or other immigrants who are not yet believers.

(2) Mission *through* the diaspora: immigrant believers reach out to those in their own ethnic group, both in the host country and sometimes beyond, by returning as missionaries.

(3) Mission *by* and *beyond* the diaspora: immigrant believers share the gospel cross-culturally, with those in the host country or in other contexts.

In our work with World Relief, empowering local churches to serve resettled refugees, we have seen each of these dynamics at play. The arrival of non-Christian (or nominally Christian) refugees is actually an invitation for local churches to love, welcome, and as we build relationships, share the hope of the gospel. By one analysis, more unreached people groups live *within the boundaries of the United States*—361—than in any other country besides India and China.[29] Many of those groups come to the United States as refugees.

In Somalia, for example, 99.8 percent of the population is Muslims; less than 0.1 percent is Christian, making it one of the least-reached countries.[30] But in recent years, an average of six thousand Somali refugees annually have been admitted to the United States. One man, who had resettled to suburban Chicago, recently visited his neighbor and English teacher, Josh, with a request. In his refugee camp in Ethiopia, he had heard about a movie called *The Jesus Film*. He wondered if Josh could help him locate it in his language. In response to his questions, Josh got to share the good news: that God so loved the world that He sent His Son, Jesus, to take the sins of all who choose to believe in Him, reconciling us to God, and giving us the hope of eternal life (John 3:16).

World Relief is an unabashedly evangelical organization. We believe in evangelism—an open invitation to a personal relationship with Jesus—but we reject proselytism, which is not synonymous. In fact, proselytism, which is a coercive effort to convert someone, is in many ways counter to evangelism. Evangelism must never pressure or compel; it should never qualify service, acceptance, or compassion based on anyone's response to faith. Theologian John Stott described proselytism as "unworthy witness," which occurs whenever our motives, our methods, or our message are unworthy.[31] As evangelicals, to quote the Lausanne Movement, "while the nature of our faith requires us to share the gospel with others, our practice is to make an open and honest statement of it, which leaves the hearers entirely free to make up their own minds about it. We wish to be sensitive to those of other faiths, and we reject any approach that seeks to force conversion on them."[32]

In serving refugees who have fled traumatizing situations of persecution, it is vital that we be particularly sensitive to avoid even implied expectations of religious conformity. As we welcome and serve refugees, we have many opportunities "to give an answer to everyone who asks you to give the reason for the hope that you have," but we must always do so "with gentleness and respect" (1 Peter 3:15). Whether a refugee is a Christian or not, and whether we believe they may *ever* become a Christian or not, our firm belief at World Relief is that we should provide the same caring service. But as our staff and local church-based volunteers build relationships with those whom we serve, the refugees very often ask what motivates our kindness, and we have seen many subsequently choose to follow Jesus.

We should not presume that once non-Christian refugees have been resettled to a majority-Christian country, they will automatically encounter the gospel. At present, fully 60 percent of people of non-Christian religious traditions residing in North America— most of them foreign-born—say that they do not personally know a Christian.[33] Not that they have never read the Bible or been to church, but that they do not even *know* a Christian. That makes sense when we realize that only 27 percent of white evangelicals in the United States personally know a Muslim, and even fewer know someone who is Hindu or Buddhist.[34] As missions pastor J. D. Payne notes, "Something is missionally malignant whenever we are willing to make great sacrifices to travel the world to reach a people group but are not willing to walk across the street."[35]

We should also recognize, as theologian Juan Martinez notes, that immigrants are not merely *objects* of mission but also *agents* of mission.[36] Many are already strong believers, and many others, who are not *yet* Christians, could, once they choose to follow Jesus and have their lives directed by the Holy Spirit, become the most effective evangelists to those of their own ethnic communities and beyond. For example, at New City Fellowship in St. Louis, Missouri, connections to refugees and other immigrants locally have revolutionized their global mission efforts, as immigrants have served as cultural brokers back to their homelands, including Togo, Burma, Pakistan, and the Democratic Republic of the Congo.

What if the Muslim refugee entering the United States from Syria today were to become the next Billy Graham?[37] Stranger things have happened: to paraphrase the late theologian Carl F. Henry, few would have predicted that God would use Saul of Tarsus, who persecuted the church with a zeal that rivals ISIS today, to be among the greatest apostles, or agnostic academic C. S. Lewis to be among the greatest apologists of the twentieth century.[38]

As refugees and other immigrants settle throughout the United States—not just in the historic immigrant gateway cities such as New York, Miami, Los Angeles, and Chicago, but also in suburbs and small cities and towns—the missional implications for the church are significant, as scholars from a range of Christian traditions have witnessed. Southern Baptist theologian Albert Mohler argues that "we've never faced such a Great Commission responsibility."[39]

As some Christian leaders fret that younger Americans are leaving the church,[40] immigrant communities may present an antidote.

Former Reformed Church in America General Secretary Wesley Granberg-Michaelson notes: "While millennials are walking out the front door of US congregations, immigrant Christian communities are appearing right around the corner, and sometimes knocking at the back door. And they may hold the key to vitality for American Christianity."[41]

Similarly, Joseph Castleberry, a Pentecostal scholar, argues that the arrival of refugees and other immigrants represents "the most realistic hope for revival and awakening in our time."[42] Wesleyan missiologist Timothy Tennent, noting that the percentage of immigrants in North America who either *arrive as* or *become* Christians is significantly higher than the Christian share of the native-born US population, argues, "We shouldn't see [immigration] as something that threatens us."[43]

Unfortunately, while some local churches are engaging this missional moment, many others are missing it. A 2016 LifeWay Research survey found that just 8 percent of Protestant US pastors said their churches are currently involved in serving refugees locally.[44] When asked their views of immigrants arriving in the United States, a majority of evangelical Christians had something negative to say—that immigrants represented a "threat" or a "burden" in some way—but only a minority said that the arrival of immigrants represented an "opportunity to introduce them to Jesus Christ."[45] We risk ignoring a divine mandate if our sole priorities are safety, comfort, and convenience.

God is working, as He has been throughout history, through the migration of refugees and other migrants. If we are to join Him in that mission, we need to recognize that "the harvest is plentiful" (Matt. 9:37), and that will require us to commit to thinking biblically—not merely politically or economically—about the reality of refugees.

CHAPTER 3

THE HUMAN FACE OF FORCED MIGRATION:

THE POWER OF A STORY

In the first and second books of the Bible, respectively, we find two competing models of how to respond to foreigners. In contrast to the pharaoh described in Genesis, who sought and benefited from the dream-interpretation and famine-management skills of an immigrant named Joseph, the pharaoh depicted in Exodus saw foreigners distinctly as a threat. He believed that the Hebrews, the descendants of Joseph and his brothers, had "become far too numerous" and presented a risk to national security (Ex. 1:9). Eventually this pharaoh's fear led him to take drastic action to eliminate this "problem," instituting a genocide of all young Hebrew boys.

It is instructive that the first descriptor of this pharaoh is that he "did not know Joseph" (Ex. 1:8 ESV). His predecessor knew Joseph personally—his name, his face, his potential—and, as far as the text describes, was never moved by fear to act with hostility toward foreigners. To the contrary, when Joseph's father and brothers fled famine and sought to settle in Egypt, that pharaoh personally welcomed them and offered them "the best part of the land" (Gen. 47:6). But the pharaoh in Exodus did *not* know the Hebrews' individual names, faces, and stories: he feared them as a group, without knowing their particularities. When you know someone personally, writes psychologist Mary Pipher, "that person stops being a stereotype and becomes a complex human being like oneself."[1]

Through our work with World Relief, each of us has had the privilege to know many refugees. These relationships have transformed our thinking. For us, the word *refugee* is no longer an abstract descriptor, or merely a legal designation, or a statistic: he or she is our neighbor, colleague, friend, or even family.

As refugees and other immigrants arrive into our communities, we can choose, like the pharaoh of Exodus, to see them as a potential threat. The better response, we believe, is to get to know them individually, and to remember, as we hear their distinct stories and begin to appreciate their particular personalities, that each is deeply loved by God.

Building relationships helps us to avoid lumping all refugees into one category of our understanding. As novelist Chimamanda Ngozi Adichie observes, there is danger in hearing only "a single story."[2] For some, the single story they associate with the idea of *refugee* is that they are dangerous. Or helpless. Or terrorists. Or perhaps flag-waving Americanized successes. Whatever the single story we have heard, it cannot accurately or fairly describe the realities of the millions of individual human beings in our world who have fled their homelands. Each of them, as every human being, is both made in the image of God with inherent dignity and yet also imperfect. No one story can speak for all refugees, or for all who share their country of origin, their religion, or even their surname.

With that in mind and to give you a sense of the diversity of the refugee experience, in this chapter we introduce five individuals, each of whom has been resettled into the United States. As you read each story, consider who they are in light of God's love for them and of our biblical responsibility toward foreigners. We hope that they will help you to put names to an often-stigmatized term and compel *you* to reach out to refugees in your community.

RAMI: A SYRIAN VETERINARIAN

Rami and his three siblings grew up in a middle-class Sunni Muslim home in Homs, Syria, the children of a taxi driver and a stay-at-home mom. Following high school, he found work finishing granite countertops while he studied veterinary science. After earning his associate's degree, Rami found work in his field, caring for chickens. Eventually he married and started a family. He describes his life in Syria as "wonderful." It was "a very safe place," where families would go out on the street and talk to their neighbors. Their life was "beautiful," Rami remembers—until the spring of 2011, when his country erupted into civil war. "In April 2011, everything changed," he says, his voice softening somberly.

Syria's civil war emerged amid a larger regional context. In 2010, a female Tunisian police officer slapped twenty-six-year-old Mohamed Bouazizi for selling vegetables without a permit, then confiscated his wooden cart. Mohamed, who was supporting his widowed mother and six siblings, set himself on fire in protest. Video of the humiliating event, captured on a cellphone, resonated with millions of people across the Middle East and North Africa, eager to find their voice and freedom. The Arab Spring had begun.

While Tunisia went through a relatively peaceful transition to democracy, the government of Syrian president Bashar al-Assad met the initially nonviolent protests in Syria with deadly force. That conflict sparked a civil war that has pitted the Assad government against various rebel groups, most of them composed of Sunni Muslims,[3] who make up the majority of Syrians. Various other countries— including Iran, Saudi Arabia, Turkey, Russia, and the United States—have backed different sides in the war, which has already claimed more than 250,000 lives, one-third or more of them civilians.[4] While responsible for only a small fraction of the overall deaths, one particular rebel group, the so-called Islamic State, or ISIS, which emerged in 2013, has used headline-grabbing brutal methods and has particularly targeted Christians and other religious minorities.[5]

The Syrian Refugee Crisis Map

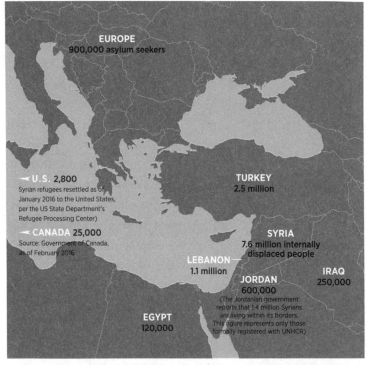

Except where noted, numbers are estimates of Syrian refugees/asylum seekers from the United Nations High Commissioner for Refugees as of December 2015 (http://data.unhcr.org/syrianrefugees/regional.php).

More than twelve million Syrians—half the total prewar population—have fled their homes to escape this violence. More than four million of those have become refugees outside of the nation's borders, most of them fleeing to neighboring Turkey, Lebanon, and Jordan. While several hundred thousand have continued on to seek asylum in Europe and a much smaller number have been resettled to Canada or the United States, the vast majority of Syrian refugees remain in those neighboring countries.

Among those forced to escape were Rami and his family. When violence first erupted in Homs, Rami tried to stay, in part because his father, suffering from kidney disease, needed regular dialysis. But as rocket fire intensified, once hitting very close to their house with a horrific noise, it became risky even to leave their home. Eventually, electricity was cut off and bread and water became scarce. Rami, his wife, and his children fled—first to another city within Syria, then, in 2012, to Turkey.

Shortly after arriving in Turkey, Rami learned that his father, unable to access medical care, had died. His grieving mother and Rami's three siblings, including a developmentally disabled brother, Raed, decided to make the perilous journey to Turkey as well.

While grateful to be safe from war, life in Turkey—where more than two million Syrians have sought refuge—was very difficult. Without knowing the Turkish language and without legal work authorization, Rami and his family found it almost impossible to sustain themselves. Rami found work repairing air conditioners, and his wife and sisters worked in a garment factory, but still their combined income was insufficient to cover food and rent, because they were paid poorly and mistreated. Unscrupulous employers in Turkey often pay extremely low wages and subject Syrian refugee employees to dangerous or demeaning working conditions, knowing that they cannot complain because they are not technically authorized to work.

Rami and his family registered with the United Nations High Commissioner for Refugees (UNHCR) shortly after arriving in Istanbul, which qualified them for some limited assistance and opened the possibility—though slim, because only a very small percentage are ultimately approved—that they could be resettled to a third country. Over the next eighteen months, they were interviewed six different times—twice by UNHCR, and then four times by various entities affiliated with the US government, which had identified Rami's family as a uniquely vulnerable case to be considered for resettlement there. The US authorities verified UNHCR's determination that Rami and his family met the legal definition of refugees *and* determined that they in no way presented a national security or public health threat to the United States.

Finally, Rami and his whole family received notice that they would be among the first Syrians—eight of 2,192 in 2015—to be resettled to the United States as refugees. Rami's sisters, brother, and mother arrived in July 2015. World Relief staff met them at O'Hare airport and took them to their new home in Aurora, Illinois. Rami and his wife and children joined them the following month.

Within a few months, with World Relief's continued help, Rami, his wife, and his sisters all found work, allowing them to cover their rent payments beyond the short window of assistance the organization could provide. Rami enrolled in English classes at the local community college, and he hopes someday to resume work using his training as a veterinarian. For now, though—while grieving all that his family has lost and ever mindful of the vast majority of Syrian people still in harm's way—he is grateful to the people of the United States for receiving him and his family. He is hopeful as he sees a safe, peaceful future for his family.

DEBORAH: PERSECUTED FOR FOLLOWING JESUS

Deborah was born in a rural farming community, without electricity, in Burma's Chin State. The Chin are one of many ethnic minorities within Burma, also known as Myanmar. Having been evangelized by American missionaries, most Chin are Baptist Christians, which make them religious minorities in their mostly Buddhist country. Their commitment to following Jesus has led to mistreatment by the Burmese government. "We, the Christians, were persecuted very badly," Deborah explains. The government expected her to produce a certain amount of food on their farm. Threatened with arrest and imprisonment if she failed to meet an unrealistic quota, Deborah, a widowed single mother, ultimately decided to flee with her nine-year-old son and six-year-old daughter, following in the footsteps of many other Chin Christian refugees. Traveling by foot and occasionally hitching a ride in a small van crammed with other refugees, they finally reached the border with Thailand. From there, Deborah used the little money she had and some jewelry to pay a guide to help them cross surreptitiously through Thailand—traveling only by night, and hiding during the day—to reach Malaysia.

Once safely in Kuala Lumpur, the largest city in Malaysia, Deborah and her kids lived with several other refugee families crammed into a small apartment with a single bathroom. Life there was also difficult: police officers would harass Chin refugees, most of whom had to work illegally to cover their basic living expenses, and threaten them if they did not pay a bribe. But Deborah found solace in a local church and a church-operated school, which provided education for her children. Having learned to speak English through her Christian college in Chin State, Deborah was able to find work as a translator with the International Rescue Committee, a global relief organization. Through those connections, she also was registered as a refugee with UNHCR.

Four years and one month after registering, in May 2013—after four different interviews, where she explained, in detail, why she had been forced to flee Burma—Deborah and her children boarded an airplane for the first time in their lives. They were heading to their new home in the United States.

After layovers in Hong Kong and Los Angeles, they landed at Chicago's O'Hare airport. Deborah's uncle, who had been previously resettled in the area, met them there and drove them to their new apartment. When she had first learned that she would be resettled to Chicago, she thought she would once again be among high-rise buildings, as she had been in Malaysia, but instead she found herself in the more spacious suburbs. As she entered their new apartment in Carol Stream, she found flowers and mangoes waiting for them on the table. At last, Deborah felt she was at home.

> More than 78,000 refugees from Burma have been admitted into the United States in the past five years, more than have been admitted from any other single country in that time frame.

The transition to the United States was not always easy, though. It took a few weeks before she would allow her children to go outside and play, the images of police harassing Chin refugees in Malaysia seared in her memory. Work is challenging, too: about three months after her arrival, Deborah found work in a warehouse, packing orders for a large supply chain company. Because the pay wasn't great, she left there and has since held two additional jobs, but most of her income goes toward covering her rent. Still, Deborah says, she is proud of herself: "I am able to pay my rent every month."

Deborah is also very involved in her church, the Falam Christian Church of Chicago, where she teaches Sunday school and preaches on some Sundays. Her faith is really what gave her the strength to seek refuge. And in each location of her journey, she notes that the one common thread has been the importance of the local church.

Today, she is particularly passionate about investing in the next generation: she has written Sunday school curriculum for children, praying that God will use it to help them, as she states, "have the mind of Jesus."

KATIE: A CHILD WHO FLED COMMUNISM

More than seventy-eight thousand refugees from Burma—most of them, like Deborah, Christians from persecuted ethnic minorities—have been admitted into the United States in the past five years, more than have been admitted from any other single country in that time frame. Between 1975 and 1995, the largest group of refugees resettled were also from Southeast Asia: more than seven hundred thousand refugees from Vietnam were resettled into the United States during that period,[6] including Katie Le, who arrived in late 1994 at the age of twelve.

Katie's father had served as an officer in South Vietnam's air force, allied with the United States. When South Vietnam fell in 1975, the new Communist government imprisoned Katie's father for six years. Katie was born a year after her father was released, but he continued to face discrimination by the government. The family moved to an isolated rural area in the southern part of Vietnam in order to escape harassment. When Katie was twelve years old, the US government offered the family the opportunity to move to the States and resettle permanently to fully escape the Communist government.

Having only lived in areas without access to electricity, clean water, or a television, Katie had only the faintest idea of what "America" was when she learned she would be living there. After a long flight to Los Angeles, she and her family met up with her aunt at the airport. Their family of five moved into a one-bedroom apartment.

Though Katie and her parents and siblings had not been religious in Vietnam, they were embraced by the congregation at Thanh Le Baptist Church, most of whom had themselves been resettled as refugees from Vietnam. Church members helped them navigate life in a new country. In time, Katie and her family became Christians as well. They still attend the same church.

Katie enrolled in school as a seventh-grader, not knowing a word of English. With the help of sympathetic teachers and countless hours of studying a dictionary, she eventually mastered the language. After finishing high school with straight As, she went on to college and, ultimately, law school.

Today, Katie is a California-licensed attorney, specializing in immigration, personal injury, and probate law. She went to law school, at first, she says, to prove to herself that she could do it. Now, as she interacts with more recent immigrants, Katie admits, "I see my family back then. I see me. I understand their struggles." She knows that recent immigrants are often not aware of their rights, and she wants to be able to help others, just as others helped her family when they had recently arrived.

PINGALA: YEARNING FOR A HOMELAND

Pingala Dhital was born in Bhutan, a small landlocked nation between India and China, in 1973. When Pingala was a teenager, the Bhutanese government began a harsh campaign known as "One Nation, One People," forcing the Lhotshampa people—who

resided in southern Bhutan, spoke Nepali, and were largely Hindu—
to adopt the language, clothing, and traditions of the government
in the north. In September 1990, sixteen-year-old Pingala joined
many others in a peaceful demonstration against this policy. The
government cracked down on what they considered an "anti-
national" protest, arresting many men and raping many women.
Within a few days of the protest, Pingala's father, who had been a
leader in the demonstration, feared he would be targeted, so he fled
across the nearby border to India.

By November 1990, the situation was only getting worse, so Pingala and her brother crossed into India in search of refuge as well,
hopeful that they would be able to return to their home within a
couple of weeks. But as the Bhutanese government forced more
people to flee—threatening them with incarceration if they did not
"voluntarily" emigrate—Pingala and her family stayed on in that
neighboring country.

In August 1991, the Indian government—influenced by its diplomatic relationship with Bhutan—expelled Pingala and the many
others who had fled from their homeland. Now they were forced to
live along a riverbank in Nepal. After a few months, UNHCR established several refugee camps in Nepal, which by 1992 were home to
more than one hundred thousand individuals forced out of Bhutan.
The refugees received basic materials to construct huts. Most would
stay there for more than fifteen years—unable to work, except in
"volunteer" roles that paid just a small stipend—and most always
hoping to return to Bhutan.

In 1994, four years after Pingala had become a refugee, she was
married in one of those camps. Her two children were born there.
When her grandmother died, and Pingala realized an entire generation had passed in the camps, she was devastated, as hopes of

returning to Bhutan were repeatedly dashed. "I lost everything. My future was destroyed," Pingala says.

Desperate for a better life for her children than what she could provide in a refugee camp, Pingala began to explore the possibility of being resettled elsewhere. She advocated for her people to resettle to a third country on humanitarian grounds. Though Bhutanese refugees were technically required to stay within the camps, in 2006, Pingala managed to relocate to Kathmandu, Nepal's capital city, where she made contact with the US Embassy to plead her people's case. With time, her advocacy efforts were successful: after completing screening processes with the UNHCR and the US government, on February 27, 2008, Pingala and her family were the first of more than 100,000 Bhutanese refugees to eventually be resettled into the United States, including Pingala's parents and four siblings with their families.

When Pingala learned she would be resettled to Washington, she was excited to live in the capital city. But when Pingala and her family actually arrived, a World Relief caseworker, a Nepali translator, and a few volunteers informed her that they were not in Washington, DC. They were in Spokane, in snow-covered eastern Washington State.

Still, the welcome was warm. At the apartment World Relief had set up for them, Pingala recalls, "Somebody made a big pot of lentils for us. That was so touching." Having gone through so much and been unwanted in multiple countries over almost two decades, Pingala says, it was "like coming home."

Of course, there have been challenges: Pingala's husband, who had been active in political organizing, took the first employment he could find, a very physical job in a window factory, which was a difficult adjustment. Though they spoke English, they found many in Spokane could not understand their accents. With time, though, they have felt at home in Washington State, and in 2013 were able to naturalize. "I was a refugee," Pingala says. "Now I am a US citizen."[7]

COME: THE POTENTIAL LOCKED
IN A REFUGEE CAMP

Come Nzibarega's gift for languages—he speaks five—helped land him a job, at twenty years of age, as a translator for a United Nations peacekeeping force sent to his country of Burundi. For decades Burundi has been plagued by conflicts between the nation's two largest ethnic groups. By assisting the peacekeeping force, though, the young man became a target for a rebel group.

One dark night, as Come returned from a run, a group of rebels kidnapped him and forced him into the jungle to their compound, where they beat, tortured, and interrogated him about the UN's operations. Finally, after two weeks, the UN peacekeepers raided the compound. Come was free, but not safe—and he feared that if he returned to his home, he would put his family at risk as well. Leaving behind his parents and siblings, he set out on a long journey to his uncle's house, in a different region of the country. But after he learned that the rebels had tracked him there, he decided to flee Burundi altogether.

Come ended up more than a thousand miles away in a refugee camp in Ethiopia, with a few other Burundians, but many more refugees from Somalia, Sudan, and the Democratic Republic of the Congo. He missed his family desperately, and the living conditions in the camp were deplorable, with a roof that could not keep water out when it rained. "I was hopeless," Come says. "It was really painful, because I could not see a future in front of me."

Come was also frustrated because he was not allowed to work in the camp, and he saw stifled potential in himself and all around him. "The richest places in the world are refugee camps," Come says, "because everyone is created with a purpose, with gifts, and with talents. Refugee camps are full of people who are full of potential, but who cannot use their potential. Maybe some of the problems that the world is facing right now, the solutions are in those people who are stuck in refugee camps."

Come spent his time running, which he found therapeutic. He also found community in a church within the camp, where his faith was deepened in the midst of his pain. "The church helped me a lot," Come reflects, "giving me hope that God would one day open the door for me to get out. The only thing that gave me hope and joy was knowing that God is in control of everything. And that made me strong."

Finally, after six years and as many interviews with both UNHCR and the US government, one day a friend told Come that his name was on a list of refugees selected for resettlement, which was posted outside the UNHCR office. At first, Come did not believe it—it was too good to be true, he said. But when he verified it, his name was there. "I was going to be able to fulfill my vision and my dream," he says.

Come was resettled to Spokane, Washington, on August 29, 2012. He was paired with a roommate—another refugee, from Eritrea— and with a volunteer, Jason, who became a good friend and running buddy. He found work at a Wal-Mart, working a night shift. He became involved in a local church, Genesis Church, which helped provide him with a sense of community, though he still struggles with the cultural differences: in Burundi, he says, you can stop by a friend's house at any time without scheduling something in advance, which is different from in the United States.

Come also joined the staff of World Relief Spokane, the agency that helped resettle him, where he now serves as a job developer, helping other refugees to find their first jobs. He enjoys interacting with refugees from around the world and seeing them find the dignity of working and providing for themselves, which most were denied in a refugee camp.

Come speaks publicly at every opportunity, telling his story—his testimony of how God has sustained him through incredibly difficult times—and urging anyone who will listen not to forget about those still in refugee camps. He dreams to someday host a television program, where he can provide a platform for others to tell their stories.

"I want to be a voice for refugees who are in refugee camps around the world, who are suffering," he says, "and to use my story to inspire people who are going through tough times. I truly believe that the world is changed by stories. Even Jesus used to preach using stories. I believe stories are really powerful."

WHICH PHARAOH WILL YOU BE?

In this chapter you met five refugees. While every refugee story is different, a few themes generally characterize those we have had the privilege to know. Refugees are resilient. They are, in almost all cases, grateful to the country that receives them. They lament what has been lost even while eager to succeed in a new country. They love their families and their communities, and they want a better future for their children. For all their differences, they are also a lot like each of us.

Now you have a distinct choice as you hear news reports about refugees arriving to your community: Will you, like the pharaoh of Exodus, hear about masses of people and presume they are a threat? Or rather than labeling them from a distance, will you get to know them?[8] The pharaoh who saw Joseph's potential and welcomed his family ended up being blessed in return—as did the entire country of Egypt, which was spared the worst effects of a famine because God providentially placed this particular foreigner in their land, subverting the unjust circumstances that compelled his migration.

Having served hundreds of thousands of refugees since the late 1970s, we and our colleagues at World Relief have come to the conclusion that they are a blessing—to us as individuals, to the church, and to our nation.

CHAPTER 4

NO FEAR IN LOVE:

GRAPPLING WITH GENUINE CONCERNS OVER REFUGEE RESETTLEMENT

Elena, a mother in Modesto, California, is probably representative of many American Christians. As she saw news reports
about a global refugee crisis—with hundreds of thousands risking
their lives to find safety in Europe, and others being resettled into
her own country—she felt conflicted. She could not help but feel
compassion, and yet she was also uncomfortable and hesitant, especially with the idea of Middle Eastern refugees being resettled into
her town. With nearly constant reminders of the risk of terrorism,
how could she be sure she would not put herself and her family at
risk by welcoming them?

Many Americans share Elena's deep ambivalence toward refugees
and refugee resettlement. They are moved by their plight, yet also fear-
ful that welcoming refugees might be naïve, imprudent, even dangerous. Questions about the wisdom of welcoming refugees—given the
various economic, legal, security, cultural, and religious concerns—
are legitimate. So let's explore some of those common concerns.

"AREN'T THEY A DRAIN ON OUR ALREADY-STRUGGLING ECONOMY?"

What's the most important voting issue to evangelical Christians? It's not refugee or immigration policy. Nor is it abortion, marriage, or religious liberty. It's not concern for the poor, nor foreign policy. Like other Americans—at least according to several recent surveys—the most important issue to evangelical Christians is the economy.[1]

It's natural, especially as so many struggle to make ends meet on a monthly basis, to be concerned with the economic impact of refugees. We want to be compassionate as a nation and as individuals, but can we afford to? Don't we have enough troubles of our own—including assisting the unemployed, the elderly, the disabled, veterans, and other US citizens—without caring for those displaced from other countries?

> While many Americans believe that refugees and immigrants more broadly are a "drain" on the economy, economists almost universally reach a different conclusion.

The presumption at the root of these concerns is that resettling refugees means a net *cost* to the national economy of the country that receives them. Interestingly, while many Americans believe that refugees and immigrants more broadly are a "drain" on the economy, economists almost universally reach a different conclusion.

That's because the economic research on issues of immigration generally finds that immigrants have a net positive impact on the country that receives them. In part, that is because immigrants are consumers—paying rent or a mortgage, buying food, cars, cellphones, and laundry detergent, just like the rest of us—and that purchasing power leads to increased profits for American businesses and generates further employment.

Most economists also agree that the average American-born worker actually sees their wages *positively* impacted by the presence of immigrants, because most immigrants tend to work in fields that *complement*, rather than compete with, the work that most Americans are either willing or able to do. For example, an Iowa dairy farmer recently shared with one of us that he has been able to stay in his family's business only because immigrants are willing to accept work milking cows; very few native-born Iowans apply when he has job openings. But because those immigrants do that work, a nearby ice cream factory still has access to milk with limited transportation costs and is able to employ many US citizens. Without the immigrant workers, that ice cream factory would likely also relocate, and many American citizens would be out of work. There is less unanimity among economists on the question of whether the impact on the wages of the least-educated American workers—who are usually closer to competing with less-educated immigrants—is positive or negative, but most economists agree any such impact is minimal.[2]

Economists also find that immigrants positively impact the fiscal well-being of the nation that receives them, paying more in taxes than they receive in benefits.[3] In the United States, for example, the American Enterprise Institute found that, in 2009, the average immigrant adult paid $7,826 in state, federal, and payroll taxes, while their families received $4,422 worth of major governmental services and benefits (including, but not limited to, Social Security, welfare programs, food stamps, unemployment insurance, Medicaid, and Medicare).[4]

There has been less research on the specific impact of *refugees* (as opposed to immigrants generally—we'll discuss more of these distinctions in chapter 6) on the economy, but significant evidence shows that countries that welcome refugees are actually likely to benefit economically as a result. For example, as millions of refugees have fled Syria in the past five years, Lebanon, Turkey, and Jordan—the countries that have received the vast majority of them—have seen their national economies grow at the fastest rates in many years. In Germany —where researchers fret that, with birthrates among the lowest in the world, the ratio of workers to retirees is declining to levels that imperil the country's pension system—Chancellor Angela Merkel's commitment to receive eight hundred thousand or more Syrian asylum seekers may be driven by compassion, but it is also a shrewd long-term economic decision.[6]

> One study, focused on refugees in the Utica, New York, area, found that the fiscal impacts of refugees became positive, on average, thirteen years after the refugee's arrival— and stayed positive, such that the net fiscal impact was positive.

In the United States, research by University of Texas economist Kalena Cortes finds that, in the long term (ten to fifteen years after resettlement), those who came to the United States as refugees actually fared better economically—earning more and working more hours—than immigrants who came for other reasons.[7] And most refugees *are* working: in fact, refugee men are more likely to be employed than US citizen men, while refugee and US citizen women work at the same rates.[8]

Unlike immigrants who are present unlawfully or those who come lawfully through a family or employer sponsor, refugees generally qualify for public benefits when they first arrive, so more costs are associated up front with refugees than with other immigrants. There are governmental costs for the resettlement services they receive as well. So for the first few years, the fiscal costs may be greater than their contributions back into the economy. One study, focused on refugees in the Utica, New York, area, found that the fiscal impacts of refugees—comparing governmental expenditures on their behalf (for public benefits, education, and public health insurance) as well as new governmental revenue from taxes they paid—became positive, on average, thirteen years after the refugee's arrival—and stayed positive, such that the net fiscal impact was positive.[9]

One predictor of how refugees arriving today might fare long term is to look at those who have arrived in the past. From 1975 to 1984, beginning with the fall of Saigon, the United States accepted hundreds of thousands of refugees from Vietnam, and the population of Vietnamese Americans increased exponentially. Several decades later, Vietnamese Americans are, overall, an economic success story: as compared to Americans as a whole, they are more likely to be employed and have slightly *higher* household incomes, on average.[10] And such economic success came not at the expense of American workers but often through entrepreneurship. For example, as economists Maya Federman, David Harrington, and Kathy Krynski note, Vietnamese refugees popularized the walk-in nail salon; they "found many new nails to polish" by expanding an industry that had once been only for the very wealthy and making it accessible to many average Americans, generating new jobs and wealth in the process.[11]

Indeed, many refugees are entrepreneurial. Bhim Thapa is one example. Having spent most of his life in a refugee camp in Nepal, Bhim achieved one of his life goals in 2013 when he opened Namaste Foods, a small grocery store serving both fellow Bhutanese refugees and the larger community of Wheaton, Illinois. Similarly, Olga and Anatoliy Filenko, who fled persecution in Ukraine and were resettled in Spokane, Washington, own Kiev Market, which they have expanded into three locations, specializing in baked goods, smoked fish and meats, produce, and other foods for the eastern European community. Stories like these are common in refugee communities: for example, a recent study of refugees in central Ohio found that they were about twice as likely as the general population to own a business.[12] In the Columbus area, there are 873 refugee-owned businesses, which collectively employ 3,960 workers.[13]

At least one refugee's "small business" has gone on to become the world's most valuable company[14] and employs tens of thousands: Google cofounder Sergey Brin fled anti-Semitism in the Soviet Union as a six-year-old and, with his family, was resettled in the United States by the Hebrew Immigrant Aid Society.[15]

The economic data is clear: refugees present an economic opportunity for countries willing to receive them. But even if they did not, our response as Christ followers cannot be a mere cost-benefit calculation. We are called to love our neighbors, even if—as it was for the "Good Samaritan" in Jesus' parable—this costs us something.

"WHAT PART OF ILLEGAL DON'T YOU UNDERSTAND?"

Another common reservation about refugee resettlement is rooted in respect for the rule of law. As Christians we are called to "be subject to the governing authorities" (Rom. 13:1), so we certainly ought not to dismiss what the law says on these matters.

When it comes to refugees resettled, the question of legality is not complicated: refugees are selected by the US State Department and admitted by the US Department of Homeland Security under the authority of the Refugee Act of 1980. Under the law, they have full legal status from the day they arrive, with authorization to work and the right to move elsewhere within the country should they choose to do so, just like any US citizen. Although a refugee can still be deported so long as they remain noncitizens (if, for example, they are convicted of a particular criminal offense), their presence here is entirely lawful. One year after arrival, they can and should apply for their Lawful Permanent Resident status (the "green card"), and after five years they generally become eligible to apply to become US citizens.

While the United States does have a significant number of immigrants who are present unlawfully—who are undocumented, either having overstayed a temporary visa or crossed a border illegally—that is really a separate question from refugee resettlement. The three of us are sympathetic to the plight of undocumented immigrants. Their circumstances within this country, and the dynamics under which they made difficult decisions to migrate, are complex. Some may have been motivated only by economic factors, but others were also fleeing violence or persecution, even if they have never been legally recognized as refugees.

> More Christians were beneficiaries of the US refugee resettlement program in the last decade than those of any other world religion.

The legal questions regarding refugees who are admitted through the US refugee resettlement program, though, are actually much more straightforward: they are lawfully admitted. Old Testament scholar James Hoffmeier, who argues that the Bible would have us firmly distinguish between immigrants with and without legal status, nevertheless affirms that "governments should treat the legal alien in the same manner it does citizens."[16]

"CAN'T WE JUST TAKE CHRISTIAN REFUGEES?"

Based on the very selective coverage of refugee issues in certain media outlets, one might reasonably presume that all refugees to the United States are military-aged Muslim men from the Middle East—and that a high percentage of them are terrorists.

Each element of that statement, it turns out, is inaccurate. Over the past decade, only about 27 percent of refugees admitted were from the Middle East. The top country of origin for refugees during this period was Burma, in Southeast Asia, and more than 70 percent of those refugees were persecuted Christian minorities.[17] In fact, from all countries, more Christians were beneficiaries of the US refugee resettlement program in the last decade than those of any other world religion.[18]

If we focus solely on the 168,242 refugees who *were* admitted from the Middle East between 2006 and 2015, 61 percent were women or children under the age of fourteen. Just over 50 percent of those were Muslims, but fully 39 percent were Christians, a far higher percentage than the share of those still in the region who identify as Christians, because Christians (along with other religious minorities) have been particularly persecuted.[19]

While the 291,285 Christians admitted account for the plurality of those brought through the US refugee resettlement program between 2006 and 2015, many non-Christians came to the United States as refugees during that time period as well, including 52,423 Hindus (almost entirely from Bhutan); about 43,000 Buddhists, mostly from Burma or Bhutan; 2,844 Jews, mostly from Iran, Russia, or Ukraine; and about 193,000 Muslims, primarily from Iraq and Somalia.

The presence of Muslim refugees, in particular, has become a point of significant contention, with politicians and even prominent

Christian leaders arguing that Muslim refugees should be excluded altogether.

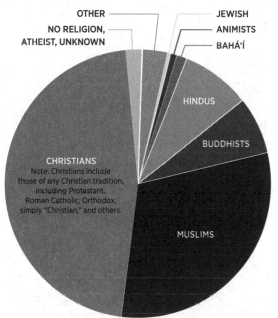

Religious Traditions of Refugees Resettled to the US, 2006 through 2015

Source: U.S. State Department Refugee Processing Center

From our perspective, Christians can err in two distinct directions as we respond to Islam. The first potential error is to believe that Christianity and Islam are essentially the same: equally valid paths to the same God. As any Muslim will affirm for you, though, while Muslims *do* revere Jesus as a prophet, they do not believe He is God's Son, nor do they believe in His resurrection, which for us as Christians is an essential element of our faith: "If Christ has not been raised, your faith is futile" (1 Cor. 15:17). We believe, as Scripture teaches clearly, that "salvation is found in no one else [besides Christ], for there is no other name under heaven given to mankind by which we must be saved" (Acts 4:12). As Christians we believe that we can never be good enough to be reconciled to God but are saved only by grace—by receiving God's forgiveness—and only through Jesus. "No one comes to the Father except through me" (John 14:6), Jesus said, and so we want as many as possible to be reconciled to God through a life-transforming encounter with Jesus.

An equally common mistake, though, is to view Muslims as enemies to be feared. Each of us—and especially Issam, who grew up in a predominately Muslim country—has many friends who are Muslims. In our experience, the vast majority of Muslim refugees are kind people, committed to their families, and grateful to the country that has received them. Polls of Muslim Americans find that the vast majority reject extremism and violence,[20] and that has certainly been our overwhelming experience.

We do not appreciate it when a media personality describes the beliefs of Christians in a way that we believe is a false caricature of biblical Christianity. Too often, based on the actions of a few, all Christians are presented as charlatans swindling poor people to buy private jets, or as ignorant simpletons skeptical of all science, or as hateful, intolerant bigots. We know that is not who we are, so we must not lump all people into stereotypes of their religion either. To apply Jesus' Golden Rule, to "do to others what you would have them do to you" (Matt. 7:12), we should extend to those of other religions the same courtesy we would like for ourselves: to be able to describe for ourselves how we understand our faith.

While acknowledging that "key aspects of the ideology of radical violent Muslim groups are indeed rooted in Islamic texts and history," scholar John Azumah, a Christian who grew up in the Muslim world, contends that it is misleading to argue that the jihadi groups represent most Muslims. He notes that Muslim leaders throughout the world view terrorist groups such as Al Qaeda and the so-called Islamic State as "heretical usurpers" and have repeatedly and publicly condemned them—even if few in the West have noticed.[21]

To "do to others what you would have them do to you" (Matt. 7:12) also means to respect and champion the religious liberty of Muslims, just as we do for ourselves as Christians. Indeed, if we fail to defend the religious liberty of others, we could imperil our own freedom: once we cede to the government (or to majority opinion) whether a particular faith and its teachings should be allowed, it is possible that the views of biblical Christians could eventually be ruled unacceptable as well. "Religious freedom for some is not religious freedom for long," warns Ed Stetzer.[22]

This is not to dismiss the reality that a small number of Muslims have engaged in horrific acts of terror in the name of Islam. However, even among the very few who might wish to do us harm because we are Christians (or because we are Americans), and whom we might reasonably classify as enemies, Jesus prohibits us from responding with hate. While the Bible makes clear that governments have the right and responsibility to execute justice against such evildoers (Rom. 13:4), Jesus also commands us to love, pray for, and provide food and drink to our enemies (see Matt. 5:44; Rom. 12:20), just as we were welcomed in by Christ when we were His enemies (Rom. 5:10).

If we respond to Muslims with love and respect, we have a remarkable opportunity to point them to Jesus. To the contrary, if we demonize or shun them, we not only risk falling into the sin of slander, we also minimize the chance that they would ever consider following Jesus, and we play into the plans of extremist groups that want marginalized Muslims to view Christians as their enemy.

The testimony of Afshin Ziafat, lead pastor of Providence Church in Frisco, Texas, is a remarkable illustration of why this approach is so essential. In 1979, Afshin's family fled persecution in Iran, where the Iranian Revolution was erupting. Upon settling in Houston—at a time when Americans were being held hostage in Iran—Afshin's family experienced further persecution: rocks thrown through their windows, tires slashed, bullying at school. But one woman, second-grader Afshin's English tutor, treated him differently: she showed Afshin kindness and love, and she gave him a Bible, which he read years later, and became a follower of Jesus. Ultimately, he became a pastor and leader reaching tens of thousands of others, including those raised as Muslims.

"Had any other American given me that New Testament," Afshin says, "I would have thrown it away, because I didn't trust them. You want to win a Muslim for Christ? I believe you've got to earn the right to be heard."[23] We earn that right by being faithful to the biblical commands to love our neighbors (Luke 10:27) and to "show proper respect to everyone" (1 Peter 2:17).

"BUT THEY WANT TO KILL US!"

For many Americans, closely tied to concerns about Muslim refugees are fears about the security risks of admitting refugees into the United States. The terrorist attacks of September 11, 2001, still haunt the memories of most citizens, with fear revived by recent jihadist terrorist attacks in Paris, San Bernardino (California), and Brussels.

None of the perpetrators in those attacks were refugees: the 9/11 hijackers all entered on nonimmigrant tourist, business, or student visas, not as refugees.[24] All of the attackers in both Paris and Brussels (whose identities have been verified as of this writing) were eventually confirmed to be European nationals, and none had been granted refugee status.[25] The attack in San Bernardino was perpetrated by a native-born US citizen and his wife, who entered on a fiancée visa.[26]

Still, many worry that a terrorist could infiltrate the US refugee resettlement program. Such concerns are understandable and we must employ prudence. But we should also not overreact in ways that would imperil the lives of legitimate refugees who have fled *from* terrorism or tyrannical governments. "Of course we want to keep terrorists out of our country, but let's not punish the victims of ISIS for the sins of ISIS," says Leith Anderson, president of the National Association of Evangelicals.[27]

In reality, the US government already does a thorough job of vetting those being considered for resettlement. After an initial screening (in most cases) by UNHCR, every individual being considered for resettlement in the United States is subjected to a lengthy vetting process that is a coordinated effort between the US Departments of State, Homeland Security, and Defense, as well as the FBI and the National Counterterrorism Center. It usually takes at least eighteen months and often much longer, involving multiple in-person interviews, interviews with third persons to verify the potential refugee's claims, biometric background checks including fingerprints and retina scans, comparison with databases of criminals and suspected terrorists, and a medical exam. Only after being cleared through this process is an airplane ticket purchased for a refugee to be admitted to the United States. If a refugee's story does not match up or cannot be verified with extensively researched country background information and intelligence sources, then the refugee is not admitted to the United States.

Notably, Europe is facing a different dynamic, with asylum seekers who have *not* yet been vetted arriving in incredible numbers at the continent's shores and borders. While some degree of background

> ISIS fighters or terrorists who are intent on attacking US soil have myriad other options for doing so that are all cheaper, easier, and more likely to succeed than sneaking in through the heavily guarded refugee gate.

check can be done upon arrival, it is not the thorough and highly selective process that the United States employs, because, unlike Europe, America is separated by an ocean from the conflicts in countries like Syria, Iraq, Afghanistan, and Eritrea.

While acknowledging that intelligence is never perfect and there is never an absolute guarantee of security, FBI Director James Comey has said that his agency has an effective process with intelligence and other agencies to conduct vetting of refugees.[28] In fact, the vetting process for refugees is much more strenuous than that to which any other category of immigrant or visitor to the United States is subjected.[29] It would not be logical for a would-be terrorist to try to enter the United States as one of approximately eighty-five thousand refugees admitted annually rather than as one of the nearly seventy *million* visitors who come into the country each year and are subjected to a much less thorough screening process.[30] Researcher Alex Nowrasteh, who analyzed the statistical probabilities of a terrorist gaining access to this country through the refugee resettlement program, concludes: "ISIS fighters or terrorists who are intent on attacking US soil have myriad other options for doing so that are all cheaper, easier, and more likely to succeed than sneaking in through the heavily guarded refugee gate."[31]

In fact, with more than three million refugees admitted through the US refugee resettlement program since the late 1970s, none has

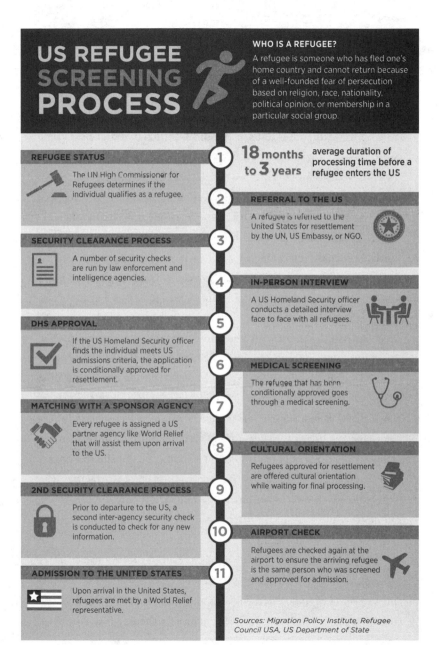

US REFUGEE SCREENING PROCESS

WHO IS A REFUGEE?
A refugee is someone who has fled one's home country and cannot return because of a well-founded fear of persecution based on religion, race, nationality, political opinion, or membership in a particular social group.

1 — **18 months to 3 years** average duration of processing time before a refugee enters the US

REFUGEE STATUS
The UN High Commissioner for Refugees determines if the individual qualifies as a refugee.

2 — **REFERRAL TO THE US**
A refugee is referred to the United States for resettlement by the UN, US Embassy, or NGO.

3

SECURITY CLEARANCE PROCESS
A number of security checks are run by law enforcement and intelligence agencies.

4 — **IN-PERSON INTERVIEW**
A US Homeland Security officer conducts a detailed interview face to face with all refugees.

5

DHS APPROVAL
If the US Homeland Security officer finds the individual meets US admissions criteria, the application is conditionally approved for resettlement.

6 — **MEDICAL SCREENING**
The refugee that has been conditionally approved goes through a medical screening.

7

MATCHING WITH A SPONSOR AGENCY
Every refugee is assigned a US partner agency like World Relief that will assist them upon arrival to the US.

8 — **CULTURAL ORIENTATION**
Refugees approved for resettlement are offered cultural orientation while waiting for final processing.

9

2ND SECURITY CLEARANCE PROCESS
Prior to departure to the US, a second inter-agency security check is conducted to check for any new information.

10 — **AIRPORT CHECK**
Refugees are checked again at the airport to ensure the arriving refugee is the same person who was screened and approved for admission.

11

ADMISSION TO THE UNITED STATES
Upon arrival in the United States, refugees are met by a World Relief representative.

Sources: Migration Policy Institute, Refugee Council USA, US Department of State

ever committed an act of terrorism within our borders, which is a testament to the rigor of the screening process. Since 2001, a very small number of individuals resettled as refugees have been convicted or charged on terrorism-related grounds, but none involved a credible threat to the United States.[32] While our biblical mandate to care for vulnerable refugees would be unchanged even if there were a terrorist attack perpetrated by a refugee, the reality is that the existing vetting process has proven remarkably effective.

Despite so much media attention on refugees, about 70 percent of terrorist attacks inspired by Islamic extremism since September 11, 2001, have been perpetrated by US citizens, most of them native-born, and many of them converts to Islam from Christian families.[33] (Notably, since 2001, there have also been as many or more deaths from terrorism tied to white supremacists and antigovernment extremists as from those claiming to be inspired by Islam.)[34] Even among those terrorists who were foreign-born, some—such as brothers Tamerlan and Dzokhar Tsarnaev, who detonated a bomb at the Boston Marathon in 2013, and whose family came on tourist visas but were eventually granted asylum status—were radicalized *inside* the United States.[35] In fact, according to an analysis by the Heritage Foundation, forty-nine of sixty Islamist-inspired terrorist plots in the United States since 9/11 "could be considered home-grown terror plots," involving either a US citizen or a foreigner who was radicalized *after* arriving in the country.[36] Jihadist terrorism, while certainly a significant threat, cannot be eliminated by preventing Muslims from entering the United States.

To the contrary, barring all Muslims from entering the country would play into the narrative of extremist groups who want *all* Muslims to think of the United States as an enemy. Conversely, if we and other majority-Christian nations champion the religious liberty of *all* people, it is more likely that the rights of Christians and other religious minorities will be reciprocally respected in Muslim-majority nations, as evidenced by the January 2016 Morocco Declaration of Muslim leaders calling for Christian minorities to be protected.[37]

While we can and should expect our government to protect American citizens, the church also has a role to play. Those most likely to be radicalized are individuals who are isolated or marginalized.[38] By proactively reaching out to Muslims (and to anyone who may not feel welcome or included in our society) with kindness, we rebut with our lives the terrorists' rhetoric that Christians and Muslims are enemies. Beyond the thorough refugee vetting process, another reason that there has never been a terrorist attack perpetrated by an individual welcomed as a refugee might be precisely that they were *welcomed*, picked up at the airport by a resettlement agency (often accompanied by volunteers from a local church or other community organization), and befriended by Americans from the day they arrived, a situation that is not offered to all immigrants.

While life always involves some risk, the security risks involved in welcoming resettled refugees are actually remarkably low, particularly compared to other threats. In fact, the threat of jihadist terrorism in the United States carried out by *anyone*—in spite of the media attention it garners—pales compared to other risks. World Vision US president Rich Stearns notes that, in recent years, more Americans have been killed by dog attacks than by Islamic extremist terrorists, but while many have called for a ban on Muslims entering the country to prevent the latter, few have called for dogs to be banned.[39] Since 9/11, more than two hundred thousand American citizens have been murdered in the United States (not including accidents or suicides), only about sixty of whom were killed by jihadist terrorists.[40]

"BE NOT AFRAID"

Elena, who felt conflicted about the arrival of refugees into her community, faced her fears: after studying the Bible and realizing how clearly Scripture commanded her to love the "foreigners in our land," she decided to put the Great Commandment into practice by volunteering with World Relief Modesto. She helped a newly arrived refugee family go grocery shopping, and then was invited in for tea. "It blessed me so much," reflects Elena, who says that getting to know these families—to see them as mothers, fathers, and children, much like her family—has removed any reservations she once had.

Indeed, the command to "be not afraid" is one of the most repeated instructions in the Bible. As we think about refugees, we believe that, while it is certainly legitimate to raise concerns and to expect our government to practice prudence, there really is not much to fear. Many of the economic, legal, religious, and security concerns about refugees are based on misconceptions, and others are overstated.

Even if welcoming refugees *were* genuinely unsafe, though, God's command would still apply. "Do not be afraid," not because there is nothing to fear but because, God says, "I am with you" (Gen. 26:24; Jer. 1:8; Matt. 28:20), because "God is our refuge and strength, an ever-present help in trouble" (Ps. 46:1).

In C. S. Lewis's mythical Narnia, Mr. Beaver is asked if the lion Aslan—the Christ-figure of the stories—is safe. "'Course he isn't safe. But he's good," he responds, and what is true of Christ is also true of the Christian life.[41] Safety is fine, but it is not—cannot—be our ultimate value if we follow Jesus. Jesus tells us explicitly, "Do not be afraid of those who kill the body but cannot kill the soul" (Matt. 10:28). We can take reasonable actions to protect ourselves and our families, but we must not allow safety to become an idol, for we follow a Lord who "laid down his life for us" (1 John 3:16) and who makes clear we must be willing to do the same to follow Him (Luke 14:26–27).

Ultimately, we welcome refugees, even when it seems scary, not because we so trust the US or any government—though the US refugee resettlement program has a strong record—but because we trust in God. We choose to love those who arrive, and "there is no fear in love [because] perfect love drives out fear" (1 John 4:18).

CHAPTER 5

FROM STRANGERS TO NEIGHBORS TO FAMILY:

UNDERSTANDING REFUGEE RESETTLEMENT

"In a simple apartment in Spartanburg, South Carolina, Ahmed brews a pot of hot tea and a plan for a new life."[1] Journalist Jamie Dean describes eloquently the optimistic prospects for Ahmed, a refugee who fled persecution in Iraq and, eventually, landed in South Carolina, welcomed by a family from a local church. He's got big plans, including pursuing further education.

A few months into his new life, the adjustment has not been entirely easy: the culture, customs, and food are profoundly different from what is "normal" to him. He still carries the trauma of the persecution that forced him to flee. And his job, in a warehouse, is strenuous and monotonous for someone who has earned a master's degree—though, says Ahmed, "if it feeds me and pays my bills, it's a great job."

In addition to the normal cultural adjustment challenges, the climate toward refugees in Spartanburg has been particularly polarized.

While scores of local churches have signed up to welcome refugees—even exceeding the number of families that the new World Relief office there has received—some others in the community have been outspokenly hostile toward refugees, especially those from Muslim countries. One local critic, at a public meeting in a high school cafeteria, called for them to be deported or, if that was not possible, shot.[2] Ahmed is aware of the attitudes a few in his new community have toward refugees like him, so he tries not to advertise his status.

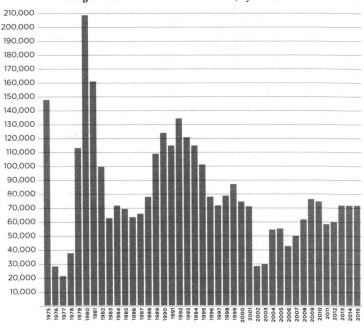

Refugees Admitted to the United States, by Fiscal Year

Source: U.S. State Department Refugee Processing Center

Ahmed is one of approximately 125,000 refugees forced to flee Iraq who have been resettled through the US refugee resettlement program since 2007, and one of approximately 600,000 refugees from all countries that have been welcomed into the country since that time. Overall, since the US refugee resettlement program was formalized with the signing of the Refugee Act of 1980, approximately three million refugees have been admitted.[3]

Refugees have come from more than one hundred different countries of origin, with a broad range of cultures, languages, religious backgrounds, and ethnicities. As we saw in chapter 3, their stories are diverse. Prior to being admitted, each has demonstrated that they meet the precise legal definition of a refugee, having fled a credible fear of persecution in their home country. But who decides which refugees should be resettled and where they will end up? And what is the process for a refugee to finally resettle here and start a new life?

THREE POSSIBLE SOLUTIONS

Resettlement to a third country like the United States is the last and, by far, least common "durable solution" for refugees.[4] Of the approximately twenty million refugees in the world in 2014, only 105,300, about one-half of 1 percent, were resettled to any new third country.[5]

The other two durable solutions are either to return—fully voluntarily, once the refugee believes it is safe—to the country of origin or to be permanently integrated into the "country of first asylum," which is usually a neighboring country. For example, approximately one million Syrian refugees have fled to Lebanon, where they now compose nearly one-quarter of the country's population. Pakistan is home to about 1.5 million refugees, primarily from neighboring Afghanistan. More than 650,000 refugees reside in Ethiopia, one of the world's poorest nations, which nevertheless has taken in many forced out by persecution in neighboring Somalia and Eritrea.[6]

These refugees are not considered "integrated" into these countries of first asylum, however, unless and until they are granted permanent legal status, with full freedom of movement, and full social integrations as residents—and perhaps, eventually, citizens—of that second country, including being granted the legal right to work and pursue economic self-sufficiency.[7]

Often, host countries are unwilling to offer this opportunity for refugees to integrate locally, and the conflicts that fueled a refugee's flight in the first place continue to make return unsafe, in some cases, for years or even decades. In those cases, third-country resettlement may be considered—but only for a select few, and it can be a very long process. The average amount of time from when a refugee first flees their country until they are finally settled in a permanent setting is seventeen years.[8]

The average amount of time from when a refugee first flees their country until they are finally settled in a permanent setting is seventeen years.

For example, in the last decade, World Relief has resettled Burundian nationals who fled—or very often, whose parents or grandparents fled—genocide in 1972. The United States accepted these individuals for resettlement after they had lived in refugee camps for decades, because ongoing tensions in Burundi prevented them from returning while Tanzania, their host country, offered no possibility of local integration.[9] Many had spent their entire lives in refugee camps.[10]

About one-third of the world's refugees spend their exile in a refugee camp, while others reside as "urban refugees" in cities or towns, usually with either the explicit or tacit consent of the host country.[11] Whether in a camp or an urban setting, most refugees are denied the dignity of a job to provide for themselves, since they are generally ineligible to work lawfully. While some may find work in the informal economy to support themselves, many others have to rely upon food rations and other humanitarian aid from the United Nations or nongovernmental organizations.

WHO GETS CHOSEN FOR RESETTLEMENT?

For the small percentage of refugees who are ultimately selected for resettlement in the United States or another country, the process usually begins with the person registering with the United Nations refugee agency, the United Nations High Commissioner for Refugees (UNHCR).

UNHCR's first role is to verify that the individual seeking registration meets all elements of the legal definition of a refugee, which they ascertain by conducting interviews with potential refugees. They note the circumstances of their flight, the reasons that they fled, and any relevant biographic details.

Once registered with UNHCR, a refugee could be considered for resettlement, but since resettlement is an option only in rare cases, UNHCR applies a number of criteria in determining which cases to refer for resettlement, prioritizing those cases that include:

- Situations when the refugee is not fully safe in the country of refuge or faces the risk of deportation to the country they have fled
- Those who have experienced torture or other violence, who could be retraumatized and/or cannot access appropriate treatment
- Those with serious medical conditions, in situations where potentially lifesaving care is inadequate or unavailable in the country of refuge

- Women and girls who are uniquely at risk of gender-based violence
- Individuals who have been separated from family members, when resettlement could result in reunification
- At-risk children, including those who are orphans or otherwise unaccompanied by parents or guardians
- Those for whom there is no foreseeable hope of local integration or voluntary return to their country of origin[12]

The common thread among these criteria is that they represent the most vulnerable cases. Resettlement is meant to be a lifeline for refugees only when all other reasonable options have been exhausted.

OVERSEAS REFUGEE PROCESSING

Once UNHCR makes a recommendation for a particular individual or family to be considered for resettlement, the US State Department (or its counterpart from other resettlement countries, such as Canada, Sweden, or Australia) begins its own process. The United States also designates certain groups of refugees who are identified directly by its government, not based on UNHCR referral.

For those being considered for resettlement to the United States, at least, the Resettlement Support Center, usually operated by a nongovernmental organization working cooperatively with the US Department of State, prepares a case file with full biographic information, initiates background checks, and helps the refugee understand the resettlement process moving forward.

From there, each refugee being considered for resettlement must undergo an interview with a US Department of Homeland Security (DHS) officer specially trained to conduct security interviews. Often a refugee must wait months or even years before they receive an interview. Officers collect biometric data used for background checks and verify that the individual indeed meets the legal definition of a refugee—checking their story with intelligence sources and with third-party interviews, as necessary—as well as that they do not present a threat to the United States. Both biometric and biographic details are compared with various databases operated by the Federal Bureau of Investigation, the National Counterterrorism Center, and the US Departments of Homeland Security, State, and Defense.

If provisionally approved, the refugee is then given a medical exam. To be eligible for resettlement, a doctor must verify that they do not present a public health threat to the United States. Assuming they pass, they are referred back to the Resettlement Support Center for cultural orientation. Each of the various security and medical checks are valid only for a limited period of time, so if one expires while waiting for another, the checks must be completed again, which is part of why this process, from referral for resettlement to departure, generally takes at least eighteen months and often much longer.

Eventually, if the refugees can complete each of these steps, the International Organization for Migration (IOM) arranges their transportation to the United States. IOM purchases the tickets——which, for a large family flying internationally, are generally thousands or even tens of thousands of dollars—but the refugee will be required to repay that interest-free loan, over time, once they are resettled. Repaying this loan helps the refugee to develop a credit history.

Finally, refugees board an airplane (or more often, a series of airplanes) and then, usually weary from travel and often experiencing a good deal of culture shock, go through one final check to verify their identity with a Customs and Border Protection agent upon arrival. From there, a representative of their resettlement agency meets them, and they begin their new lives.

THE RESETTLEMENT AGENCY

In the final stages of a refugee being processed overseas, the US State Department connects each case to one of nine nonprofit "voluntary agencies," which include World Relief.[13] Each agency has a network of local offices or affiliates where they can resettle refugees. Collectively, these nine agencies place these individuals in almost every state and the District of Columbia.

Refugees Resettled to the US in 2015

Alabama	97	Illinois	2,439	Montana	0	Rhode Island	145
Alaska	110	Indiana	1,690	Nebraska	1,068	South Carolina	249
Arizona	2,960	Iowa	815	Nevada	648	South Dakota	494
Arkansas	11	Kansas	610	New Hampshire	428	Tennessee	1,440
California	5,611	Kentucky	1,930	New Jersey	328	Texas	6,857
Colorado	1,625	Louisiana	133	New Mexico	194	Utah	1,041
Connecticut	510	Maine	402	New York	3,904	Vermont	320
Delaware	3	Maryland	1,453	North Carolina	2,369	Virginia	1,266
District of Columbia	4	Massachusetts	1,666	North Dakota	518	Washington	2,545
Florida	2,309	Michigan	2,714	Ohio	2,898	West Virginia	23
Georgia	2,803	Minnesota	2,119	Oklahoma	548	Wisconsin	1,272
Hawaii	3	Mississippi	15	Oregon	949	Wyoming	0
Idaho	961	Missouri	1,352	Pennsylvania	2,668		

Source: U.S. State Department Refugee Processing Center

On a regular basis, representatives of these nine agencies convene and divvy up among the organizations and, from there, among their respective networks, the resettlement cases arriving in the coming months. A primary factor influencing where a refugee will be resettled is if they have a connection to a family member or friend already in a particular location in the United States. Additionally, if the person has a particular health condition, he or she will be placed in a location with access to adequate health care services, or a location may be prioritized where an agency's staff have particular language skills to best serve that newly arrived refugee. Beyond that, though, there is an element of chance to where refugees arrive, as the approximately seventy thousand to eighty-five thousand refugees accepted for resettlement annually in recent years are distributed throughout the nation, some to large cities, others to small cities and suburbs.

One key function of the resettlement agency is to ensure that the larger community understands and is able to help integrate refugees. Both before beginning resettlement in a new location and on an ongoing basis, the resettlement agency consults with local social service providers, businesses who will serve as potential employers, schools, law enforcement, government officials, and religious organizations.

> The goal is for all employable adults to be employed and financially self-sufficient, covering their own rent and other basic living expenses, within several months of arrival.

Once a refugee arrives, the resettlement agency is responsible for providing a basic level of care and support, meeting basic needs for the first few months after arrival, and then equipping them to be self-sufficient members of the community. The resettlement agency will also have furnished housing ready for each arrival, ensure that a culturally appropriate first meal is waiting for them, and will meet and welcome them at the airport (with coats, if they are arriving into a cold climate in the winter). In the first several days, the caseworker will take the family to a medical screening and help them to apply for their Social Security cards as well as food stamps and other transitional public benefits that will help sustain them during the initial resettlement period.

The resettlement agency staff also helps kids—about one-third of all refugees resettled here are under eighteen years of age[14]—to enroll in school, while adults are connected to opportunities for cultural orientation, English language instruction, and job skills training, then assisted in finding their first job. The goal is for all employable adults—generally everyone except for children, the elderly, and the disabled—to be employed and financially self-sufficient, covering their own rent and other basic living expenses, within several months of arrival.

Refugee resettlement agencies are funded through a combination of public and private sources. The US Department of State provides a fixed per capita grant of $2,025 per refugee,[15] most of which is spent on direct expenses, including the cost of renting an apartment or other housing for the first few months as well as purchasing furnishings and other household materials. The remainder of the grant covers the agency's staffing costs, including a caseworker. Resettlement agencies generally receive additional funding from the US Department of Health and Human Services, a modest portion of the repayment of the refugee's travel loan, and, in some (but not all) states, from state or local governmental grants.

However, the public funds used to support these resettlement activities do not cover the actual total costs of resettlement and integration. Resettlement agencies rely upon private fundraising from churches, foundations, and individuals to defray their costs. They also depend upon donations of noncash items, such as furniture, dishes, pots and pans, and other household items to furnish each new arrival's home. At World Relief, we ask local churches and community groups to assemble a "Welcome Kit" that includes many of these key items.

Finally, in any resettlement agency, volunteers play a crucial role both in providing supplemental services and, perhaps more importantly, as friends. At World Relief, in particular, our mission is not merely to serve refugees well—though we certainly aim to do that—but "to empower the local church to serve the vulnerable." We can only achieve our mission in intimate partnership with local churches wherever we resettle refugees. Teams and individuals from churches provide a deeper level of relational connection to each family than our staff alone are able to provide.

BEYOND THE UNITED STATES

While our expertise is in the US refugee resettlement program, several other countries also resettle refugees, generally also taking referrals from UNHCR.

Canada, for example, took in 12,300 refugees in 2014,[16] but late in 2015—in response to the Syrian refugee crisis and as part of a campaign promise from newly elected prime minister Justin Trudeau—the country committed to take in twenty-five thousand Syrian refugees, providing privately chartered flights to bring hundreds of refugees per day into Toronto and Montreal, beginning in December 2015.[17]

Unlike in the United States, where all refugee resettlement occurs through a partnership between the government and faith-based or other nonprofit organizations (and where it is *not* possible for a church to sponsor a specific refugee abroad to be resettled), Canada has two distinct systems: a governmentally funded and operated resettlement program and a separate, privately funded system, where a local church, a community organization, or any other group of Canadians can propose and sponsor a particular refugee family, contributing about C $27,000 (about US $19,500) for a family of four. As in the United States, these community groups then play a significant role in helping the refugee family to integrate, while those sponsored by the government are served primarily through governmental agencies. Various denominations and parachurch ministries help to connect local congregations with refugee sponsorship opportunities.

Australia also resettles a significant number of refugees each year, including more than thirteen thousand in 2013.[18] Refugee resettlement and integration services are generally provided by nonprofit organizations, some of them faith-based.[19] A significant number of people also seek asylum in Australia each year, but the Australian government generally detains them offshore through a controversial policy designed to discourage people from seeking asylum in Australia.[20]

In Europe, the vast majority of those who have fled persecution arrive not through a resettlement program but as asylum seekers; more than one million individuals sought asylum in Europe in 2015.[21] However, several European countries do accept a small number of resettled refugees, particularly the Nordic countries. Collectively, the European Union has admitted about five thousand resettled refugees annually in recent years, plus slightly more than one thousand refugees resettled in Norway.[22]

FROM HOSTILITY, TO HOSPITALITY, TO HOUSEHOLD

Ahmed is an example of the strengths of refugee resettlement. While there has been hostility to refugee resettlement among a small but vocal group of residents in Spartanburg, South Carolina, the overwhelming response, led by local churches, has been one of genuine *hospitality*.

In the minds of most Americans, as author Christine Pohl clarifies, hospitality "chiefly refers to the entertainment of one's acquaintances at home and to the hospitality industry's provision of service through hotels and restaurants."[23] When we are commanded in the Scriptures to "practice hospitality"—the word used in Romans 12:13 is *philoxenia*—it literally means to "practice loving strangers." Loving and welcoming our friends is insufficient—even the tax collectors and sinners of Jesus' day did that (Matt. 5:46–47). Jesus called strangers our neighbors, defying the conventional thinking of both His time and ours (Matt. 25:31). According to Tim Keller, the strangers whom Jesus talked about

> were immigrants and refugees, and they were . . . to be "invited in." They were not merely to be sent to a shelter but were to be welcomed into the disciples' homes and lives and, it is implied, given advocacy, friendship, and the basics for pursuing a new life in society.[24]

But even hospitality is not the end goal, says theologian Soong-Chan Rah: "We need to move from hostility, to hospitality, and then to household . . . to becoming family."[25] We begin by loving strangers, but soon they are not strangers. They are neighbors, and ultimately, we hope, brothers and sisters.

Ahmed came to the United States by himself, without family, but has been embraced by volunteers from a local church. "They are my family now," he says.[26] Ahmed, who comes from a Muslim background, has been attending church regularly and has joined a small group. While his new Christian friends have made clear that their care for him is unconditional—he is under no pressure to embrace Christianity—he is drawn to Jesus by the kindness displayed by these new friends.

While the metaphor does not transfer perfectly, that progression from strangers, to neighbors, to family is paralleled in the refugee resettlement process for a nation. Refugees arrive, are embraced by local communities, and integrate into the fabric of the community and the nation. That does not mean they abandon their culture or language or foods, but over time, they integrate those unique elements of their identity into the tapestry of the United States, which throughout its history has been enriched by the diversity of immigrants from around the world.

The legal culmination of the resettlement and integration process generally occurs approximately five years after arrival, when a refugee becomes eligible for naturalization. There are few things as inspiring as a swearing-in ceremony, where refugees—forced out of their country of birth—are recognized as new citizens, with all the rights, privileges, and responsibilities as someone born into that privileged status. The journey to freedom is complete—and the nation, as a whole, is stronger as a result as these onetime refugees invest back into the communities that have welcomed them.

CHAPTER 6

NOT (QUITE) REFUGEES:

OTHER DISPLACED PEOPLE

In January 2010, a horrific earthquake struck Haiti, killing an estimated 160,000 people and displacing more than one million others from their homes,[1] among them seventeen-year-old Douna Marcellus. Just seconds after Douna had walked out the front door to run an errand for her mother, the earthquake destroyed their home, crushing both her parents and her sisters. Desperate and homeless, Douna set out on a dangerous six-hundred-mile trip by boat to reach southern Florida. "America is a place where everybody can become someone," Douna says. "Where everyone lives like human beings." Besides, she adds, "I have nowhere else to go."[2]

The *Los Angeles Times,* which interviewed Douna, described her as a "refugee," as did various other media reports of Haitians fleeing their country after the earthquake.[3] But from a legal perspective, Douna and others like her are *not* refugees. Those caught at sea were returned to Haiti, and those apprehended upon arrival were detained and, in most cases, deported. Most of those who managed to enter the country surreptitiously became undocumented immigrants, ineligible for any legal status or benefits afforded to refugees, and at risk of deportation if caught.

Similarly, as more than one million migrants reached the shores and borders of Europe in 2015—many, but by no means all of them, fleeing Syria's civil war[4]—media reports across the globe referred to the "European refugee crisis." But from a legal perspective, it was more complicated: while many (probably most[5]) of these individuals will eventually be recognized by European governments as refugees and granted permanent asylum status, until their cases are adjudicated (a process that takes several months, depending on the country), these individuals are technically "asylum seekers." They may in fact be refugees, but no legal authority has made that determination. Others, who do not meet the legal definition of a refugee, are considered "economic migrants," fleeing poverty, perhaps, but not persecution of a sort that would legally qualify them as refugees.[6]

These legal distinctions may not matter in determining how we respond to these individuals as Christians; each is made in God's image and worthy of compassion. From a practical perspective, however, they are important. People in these different categories are treated differently, sometimes dramatically so, under the law.

Under both US and international law, a refugee is specifically defined as a person who is:

- outside his or her country of nationality or last habitual residence
- unable or unwilling to return to that country because of persecution or a well-founded fear of persecution on account of one or more of the following grounds:
  - race
  - religion
  - nationality

– membership in a particular social group

– political opinion[7]

We have already discussed how a small percentage of those who fit this definition are resettled. But there are others who are *not* technically refugees (or not yet *designated* as refugees) who still are uniquely vulnerable.

INTERNALLY DISPLACED PERSONS

Most people do not *want* to leave their homes behind, but sometimes the threat of violence leaves people with little choice. If forced to flee, most prefer to stay within the bounds of their country, where the culture and language are similar and where home remains close by so they can return. Those who flee their homes but do not cross a border are not "outside of their country of nationality," and thus are not technically refugees.[8] These individuals are referred to as "internally displaced persons." While the United Nations refugee agency estimates that 19.5 million refugees exist globally, nearly twice that many are internally displaced.

In Syria, for example, nearly four million individuals have fled the country, primarily to neighboring Turkey, Lebanon, and Jordan. But another nearly eight million have been displaced *within* the borders of Syria.[9]

As in many other situations of internal displacement, those displaced within Syria are uniquely vulnerable, because the dynamics that forced their flight—whether the Syrian government of Bashar al-Assad, the self-proclaimed Islamic State, or other rebel groups—make it extremely dangerous for relief groups to provide support within the country. The only government to which an internally displaced person can appeal for protection, in many cases, is the very government that has persecuted them, which is why some who begin as internally displaced ultimately decide they have no choice but to cross a border into a neighboring country, at which point they may qualify as a refugee.

A reporter once asked whether we, as American Christians, should help persecuted Christians in the Middle East to *stay* or, rather, help them to *leave*. The answer is not simple: our role is certainly not to second-guess the excruciatingly difficult decisions facing our brothers and sisters; it is to welcome them wherever they arrive, as we would welcome Christ Himself (Matt. 25:35).

Still, most persecuted Christians would prefer to be able to stay within their countries—particularly when their flight could mean the abandonment of a Christian presence in parts of the world where it has existed since the days of the earliest apostles. Several Catholic and Orthodox leaders in Syria have actively urged Christians to stay if at all possible, despite the risk, fearing that Syria could lose most of its historic Christian population, as has occurred in neighboring Iraq.[10]

I (Issam) have traveled back to the Middle East on several occasions to work with Syrian Christian leaders, who have made dangerous journeys out of and then back into Syria to be trained in how to help heal the trauma of the displaced people within their communities.

Similarly, in northern Iraq, our World Relief colleagues are providing "child-friendly spaces" for persecuted people who fled their homes when ISIS captured the city of Sinjar. These people include Christians, Muslims, and Yazidis, a religious minority that has been particularly targeted for extermination by ISIS and that has encountered continued discrimination even after their flight. Many of these internally displaced children have no access to education and have experienced unimaginable trauma. Without intervention, an entire generation could be lost, a normal, healthy childhood having been stolen from them by terror. These child-friendly spaces provide basic health education, life skills, and school skills as well as psychosocial support, while simultaneously offering trauma support for their mothers and older sisters.

While internally displaced people remain distant from us, churches in the West can come alongside local churches and relief organizations in countries such as Iraq, South Sudan, the Democratic Republic of the Congo, and Yemen, where millions have fled their homes. By doing so, we can both express God's love by holistically meeting human needs and minimize the number who will be forced to flee their countries and become refugees.

ASYLUM SEEKERS

While internally displaced persons do not meet the legal definition of a refugee because they remain within their home country, many others do, in fact, fully meet that definition, but no authority has yet considered their case and made that determination. These people are "asylum seekers."

Both refugees and those granted asylum have fled a credible fear of persecution for one or more reasons enumerated in the law; the distinction is in *where* that determination is made. For those resettled here as refugees, our federal government makes the determination *abroad* that they are indeed refugees. When an individual arrives in the United States by means *other* than through the US refugee resettlement program, such as someone who enters on a temporary visa or who reaches the United States without any visa, they can request asylum, claiming that they fear persecution if they were to be returned to their home country.

Reaching that status, though, can be difficult, especially in the

US context. First, you cannot apply for asylum unless you reach the United States, and geography makes that extremely challenging for most in the world who have fled persecution. For those separated by an ocean, the only realistic possibility is to have a visa, which is a prerequisite to boarding a US-bound airplane, but for most of the world's population—especially those who are not wealthy or those coming from a nation in turmoil—the odds of being granted a visa to travel to the United States are nearly zero. (European countries, which have similar asylum laws but are geographically closer to conflict zones such as Syria, Iraq, and Afghanistan, receive far more asylum seekers than the States: more than one million people sought asylum in Europe in 2015 alone, about twenty-five times as many as have done so annually in the United States in recent years.)[11]

If an asylum seeker does manage to reach the United States and expresses a fear of persecution, they risk being held in a jail-like detention facility. Unbeknownst to most Americans, Congress has mandated that the US Immigration and Customs Enforcement agency maintain at least thirty-four thousand beds per night for immigrant detainees in the midst of legal proceedings, ostensibly to protect the general public from those who could be violent and to ensure that individuals show up to their hearings.[12] A significant share of those beds are occupied by individuals with pending asylum claims. In 2010, 15,768 total asylum seekers were held, on average, for about seventy-eight days.[13]

More than half of these thirty-four thousand detention beds are operated by private companies, which the federal government contracts at an average cost of $159 per person, per day.[14] Those companies, naturally, have a strong profit incentive to see *more* individuals detained. The three largest companies within the private prison industry have spent collectively more than $45 million in lobbying and campaign contributions since 2002,[15] and the number of detention beds has increased dramatically, nearly doubling since that time, including new facilities specifically for women and children detainees.[16]

Companies further maximize their profits by relying upon detainees to perform basic operational functions within detention facilities, such as cleaning and serving meals, at a pay of just $1 per day.[17] While technically not mandatory, many detainees feel compelled to "volunteer" because the facilities require them to purchase items such as pillows, ibuprofen, or telephone cards to speak to their relatives or to an attorney, often at exorbitant prices.[18]

Several independent reports have found the conditions within detention centers to be inadequate. A 2013 report from the US Commission on International Religious Freedom notes that asylum seekers are held "under inappropriate conditions" in jails and jail-like facilities.[19] The same year, a Government Accountability Office report on detention facilities found significant allegations of sexual assault and abuse against detainees, many of which had gone unreported.[20] Another report found widespread problems with access to health care within the detention centers, noting the scores of detainees who have died while in custody.[21]

One such detainee was a Baptist pastor from Haiti named Joseph Dantica, who died in a detention facility in Miami after his blood pressure medication was confiscated. After arriving here on a valid passport and visa that he had used many times before, Pastor Dantica was detained when he acknowledged to an airport immigration inspector that he wanted to seek temporary asylum because his church had been attacked by local gang members just days earlier.[22]

For those who apply affirmatively for asylum and are *not* detained, they still face a challenge: in most cases, they are ineligible for work

authorization for at least six months, and often for longer.[23] Since
they are also ineligible for public assistance, it can be very difficult to
sustain oneself while awaiting an asylum decision.

Outcomes of asylum cases are also unpredictable—even with a strong case—because they depend so entirely on the determination of a single human being. A study of asylum approvals found that, in one particular asylum office, one officer had *never* approved an asylum claim for an individual from China—the number one country of origin among asylum seekers in the United States in recent years[24]—while another officer in the same office approved more than two-thirds of claims from Chinese asylum seekers. In 2014, 84 percent of all asylum claims made before the immigration court in New York City were granted, compared to just 1 percent at the court in Atlanta, Georgia.[25] Asylum can be an arbitrary process—with life-or-death consequences. Whether an asylum seeker has legal representation (which the government does not provide) is often a major factor.

> Asylum can be an arbitrary process—with life-or-death consequences.

Overall, in recent years, around forty thousand individuals have applied for asylum and about twenty-five thousand each year have successfully received asylum here, whether from an asylum officer or in the immigration court system.[26] Having fled persecution just like those resettled as refugees, asylum seekers face all of the same challenges to adjustment—but they are not met at the airport by a resettlement agency there to assist them. At least for the first several months while they wait for their cases to be approved, they are usually ineligible either to work or to receive public assistance, while others languish in detention facilities. All of these dynamics make asylum seekers uniquely vulnerable—and a population in need of the church's support and advocacy.

OTHER IMMIGRANTS

At the church that I (Matthew) attend, a bilingual congregation in the predominantly Hispanic community where I live, many of my friends emigrated from Mexico. Most of them, if asked why they came to the United States, would cite economic factors: they were looking for a better job—and a better future for their children. Some came out of genuine desperation, faced with such extreme poverty that they did not know where their next meal would come from. Even though they may have been forced out by poverty, though, such "economic migrants" do not meet the definition of a refugee, because they are not fleeing persecution.

For at least one immigrant friend in our congregation, though, fear of violence *is* a major factor in why she is in the United States, even though she is not classified as a refugee. Gloria's hometown in Durango, Mexico, has been plagued by violence, much of it associated with brutal drug cartels. In the past decade, Gloria's ten- and twelve-year-old nieces were kidnapped and held for ransom, three other relatives were kidnapped and murdered, close friends from her church simply disappeared, and her pastor—who was deeply invested in ministering to those in and reentering society from prison—was burned to death by someone he had been trying to help.

Once able to enter the United States on a tourist visa, Gloria has not returned, in large part because she is afraid for herself and her family—even though that means she is now undocumented. She might have applied for asylum, but to be granted asylum, she would need to be able to prove a clear, specific connection between the persecution she fears and her race, religion, nationality, political opinion, or social group. In her case, that would likely have been a hard case to make because her fear, while certainly sincere, is not based on specific threats made to her, and the violence her friends and family have been victims of was not necessarily tied to their ethnicity, faith, country of origin, or political views. The most ambiguous of the five grounds of persecution enumerated in the law is "membership in a particular social group"—a ground not specifically defined by the law, and thus interpreted by the courts, sometimes in conflicting ways—but most efforts by attorneys to argue that those being targeted by gangs represented a "particular social group" have been unsuccessful in winning asylum claims in the States.[27]

> The murder rates in El Salvador, Honduras, and Guatemala were among the highest in the world in recent years; in Honduras, four out of five murders are never even investigated.

Furthermore, with few exceptions, US law requires that asylum claims must be filed within one year of arrival in the country to be considered, a deadline that has already passed in Gloria's case. Were she to apply for asylum now, she would likely be deported. Given her genuine fear of returning to Mexico—compounded by the poverty to which she would be returning and subjecting her US-born children—she feels she has no choice but to remain undocumented, praying that a visa petition filed approximately fifteen years ago by her husband's brother will one day allow them both to gain legal status, though she likely will have to wait at least four years more because of backlogs in the family-based immigration system.[28]

UNACCOMPANIED CHILDREN

The question of gang violence is particularly germane to the situation of children and teenagers who have arrived without parents at the US-Mexico border. In recent years, many (but not all) of them have fled gang-related violence in the Central American countries of Honduras, El Salvador, and Guatemala. In the summer of 2014, more than ten thousand unaccompanied minors were apprehended at the border each month, causing a media frenzy that subsided by autumn, after the Mexican government (under pressure and with assistance from the US government) began intercepting a much higher percentage of those crossing its territory, most of whom it deported back to Central America.[29]

While there were multiple reasons that these children made the decision to depart on a treacherous journey to the United States—including poverty, family reunification, and recruitment by smuggling networks—the majority cited violence as a primary reason they felt compelled to flee.[30] The murder rates in El Salvador, Honduras, and Guatemala were among the highest in the world in recent years; in Honduras, four out of five murders are never even investigated.[31] Children and teenagers were often particularly vulnerable to this violence, threatened if they did not join gangs. Many felt their only choice was to flee. As such, many argue that these individuals should be treated as refugees.[32]

The legal situation facing these young people upon arriving in the United States is complex: under a US law signed by President George W. Bush, unaccompanied minors from countries not bordering the United States who are apprehended at the border—in almost all cases, they turn themselves in to border patrol agents—are to be transferred to the custody of the US Department of Health and Human Services, which is responsible for protecting them until their

case can be adjudicated. In most cases, the children are held tempo-
rarily in shelters, usually operated by faith-based or other nonprofit
organizations, until they can be reunited with relatives already in the
United States, which the vast majority of them have. Those without
a relative may be kept in a shelter for a longer period of time or
placed into a foster care situation.

Eventually, these children are summoned to a deportation hearing,
though that can take months or even years, given a backlogged immigration court system. Their fate then—whether they will be allowed to
stay or deported to their country of origin—depends both on the mer-
its of their case and, particularly, on whether they have an attorney.
Unlike in a criminal court, those facing an immigration proceeding,
even children, are not afforded legal counsel by the government, so
only about one-third of unaccompanied minors in deportation hearings have been represented, generally by *pro bono* attorneys. Those
with an attorney were allowed to stay in 73 percent of cases, whether
by being granted asylum, a special T visa for victims of human trafficking, or some other remedy under US immigration law. But the majority who do not have an attorney are almost always ordered deported:
just 15 percent of those without representation were granted relief.[33]

Those who are ultimately deported, tragically, often face the same
violence they fled once they return to Central America. El Salvador
recently surpassed Honduras for the ignominious title of the highest
murder rate in any country outside of a war zone, twenty-five times
the murder rate of the States.[34] Tragically, based on local newspaper
reports, among those killed are at least eighty-three individuals deported from here since January 2014.[35]

DOES THE DEFINITION REALLY MATTER
TO OUR CALLING?

Among the many who have been forcibly displaced in our world, only a small share actually meet the precise legal definition of a refugee —and yet they still need refuge and a safe place to turn. As Christ followers, though, our compassion need not be limited to those who meet a particular legal definition. As Rick Warren notes, "The church must always show compassion. . . . A good Samaritan doesn't stop and ask the injured person, 'Are you legal or illegal?'"[36] Nor, we would add, "Do you meet the precise legal definition of a refugee?" While governments may need to differentiate, the church can extend compassion and love indiscriminately, because each of these individuals is made in God's image, is a person for whom Christ died, and is a neighbor whom we are called to love.

CHAPTER 7

THE CHURCH'S MOMENT:

PRACTICAL OPPORTUNITIES TO RESPOND

The plight of refugees in our world today is an unprecedented global crisis. For the church, though, it also presents a unique moment to live out our theology. The refugees of the world—some of them persecuted brothers and sisters in Christ, others of them not yet followers of Jesus—are watching how the church will respond, whether guided by faith or by fear. Let's look at a few local churches that are seizing this moment and meeting distinct needs as an expression of God's love for the displaced.

PROVIDING A WARM WELCOME

The first several months after a refugee arrives are the most intensive period of adjustment, and the role of the local church can be crucial. Our goal, at each of our World Relief offices in the United States, is for every refugee who arrives to be welcomed at the airport by a small group of committed volunteers—we call them a Good Neighbor Team—from a local church. That team commits to walking alongside that family (or individual) for at least their first six months to one year in their new country.

A Good Neighbor Team prepares to welcome a particular family even before they arrive. Because refugees generally come with significant needs—which can be overwhelming for volunteers if they are not well prepared and equipped—World Relief staff provide a thorough training for the team. We explain what to expect, the various resources and services available to refugees both from World Relief and in the larger community, some background on the country from which the family is fleeing (including any sensitive political or cultural dynamics of which the average American might not be aware), and how to be most helpful without inadvertently harming or building dependency.

The Good Neighbor Team and others from their local church will often create a Welcome Kit, consisting of dishes, pots and pans, linens, towels, cleaning supplies, and other basic household items the family will need. In some cases, they may also provide a host home for the first few days that the refugees are in the country, if the apartment is not immediately ready.

A Good Neighbor Team usually requires an organized team leader, who will be the team's primary liaison with World Relief. Other team members might play one or more additional roles, working collaboratively with World Relief staff: an English language tutor, a job skills mentor, someone to help children adjust to a new school system, a medical liaison to help make sure that doctors' appointments are not missed and to help resolve insurance questions, and a community liaison to help explain things like grocery shopping, banking, and public transportation. More important than any of these specific functions, though, the Good Neighbor Team is there to offer friendship. From the moment the family arrives at the airport, the team is there to make sure these newly arrived refugees know that they are safe, welcome, and—for some for the first time in years—home.

Though serving on a Good Neighbor Team can be intensive, many volunteers have returned time after time to serve another new family, even while maintaining relationships with families well beyond their first year in the country.

One congregation whose volunteers have welcomed refugee families for many years now is Wheaton Bible Church, located in the western suburbs of Chicago. A large nondenominational church that has been in the community for nearly a century, Wheaton Bible Church is known for its passion for overseas missions, supporting more than ninety missionaries in more than forty countries. Although individual church members have served as volunteers with refugees for decades, when Chris McElwee was asked to take on a pastoral role focused on serving and reaching those in the local community, he was only vaguely aware of what a refugee was.

> Had someone told him a few years earlier that he would have a Muslim family from Iraq sleeping in his basement, Chris would have thought that was crazy. Now it seemed strangely normal.

And he had no idea that there were approximately one hundred refugee families resettled each year through the World Relief office just up the street.

Chris remembers vividly his first experience interacting with refugees. He picked up a large Burmese family at O'Hare airport and drove them to an apartment complex just a few blocks east of their church where many refugees had been resettled. Some relatives who had arrived in the country earlier had prepared a welcome meal. With the smell of fish sauce in the air and as the sun set, Chris stood on the third-floor balcony outside of the apartment, while a dozen or more Burmese people brushed by him as they ate their meal. Beneath him, he saw a woman in traditional African dress, playing with her child. Across the way, he saw what looked like a European couple speaking a language he did not recognize—he later learned they were from Kosovo. "For a second, I literally forgot where I was," Chris said. "Everything kind of changed for me that night, and I said, 'We have got to do more. We are totally missing what is happening here right in front of us.'"

Since that time a decade ago, Wheaton Bible Church teams have welcomed and walked alongside more refugee families than Chris can remember—at least fifty, he estimates. "The primary goal," he says, "is simply to be the friend the people need when they get off that airplane. They have lots of needs, for sure, but their biggest want is just to have a friend."

These refugees have had a profound impact on Wheaton Bible Church as well. Since Iraqi refugees began arriving in the mid-2000s, several families served by Wheaton Bible Good Neighbor Teams asked if they could come to the church, particularly at Christmastime. While their team leader made clear that they were under no pressure, several families expressed a desire to attend because they had questions about Jesus. Eventually, the church established a Sunday morning Bible study in Arabic in response and, later, another in Farsi as families from Iran expressed interest. Recently, one Iraqi woman was baptized and became a member of the church.

Chris says his relationships with refugees have shaped his own perspective too. On one occasion, he and his wife hosted an Iraqi single mother and her five children in their home. Had someone told him a few years earlier that he would have a Muslim family from Iraq sleeping in his basement, Chris would have thought that was crazy. Now it seemed strangely normal.

As they befriended this family, Chris learned once more what he had observed with refugees from various countries: that, for all the differences, and not discounting the horrific realities of war and persecution that they had experienced, this mother was just like any other mother, with the same hopes, fears, and dreams for her children. "We are way more alike than we are different," Chris says.

THE CHURCH'S GENERATIONAL
IMPACT ON REFUGEES

In 1986, World Relief Nashville resettled four-year-old Thi Mitsamphanh, his six siblings, and their parents. When the family first arrived, Dave and Sandy Wood and others from Lighthouse Baptist Church met and welcomed them. Because of the team's kindness and hospitality, Thi and his family, who had been Buddhists when they fled Laos, came to faith in Christ.

Thi adjusted well to life in his adopted country, excelled in school, and went on to college. After college, following a sense that God was calling him into ministry, he moved to Memphis to attend Mid-America Baptist Theological Seminary. While there, Thi also became a pastor and church planter. The Laotian Baptist Church in Memphis had dwindled to just a few people, so Thi helped relaunch the church, which was renamed First International Baptist Church and began drawing in new people, particularly other second-generation Asian Americans.

Thi and other church members realized that their congregation was located within a few blocks of a large apartment complex where the local Catholic Charities had resettled a significant number of refugees. Many in the church who had as children experienced the challenges of adjusting to life in a new country were eager to reach out to these new neighbors, many of whom were refugees from Bhutan. After more than fifteen years in refugee camps in Nepal, several dozen families, who were mostly Hindu, had resettled in Memphis, and Thi and the First International Baptist Church welcomed them, becoming friends and mentors as they adjusted to life in the United States.

As they got to know the families, Thi and others from his church had the opportunity to share the story of the gospel with some of the families, and several became followers of Jesus. One, Prakas, became a Christian about a year after his arrival, and is now in seminary. Prakas is passionate about sharing the good news with those in his community, both locally and globally. He now serves as a pastor at First International Baptist Church—where thirty-five to forty Nepali-speakers have joined the multicultural, multilingual church, comprising about half of the congregation—and is also preparing to return to Nepal for a mission trip. What began with a church in Nashville welcoming Thi and his family is bearing fruit generations later.

BEYOND THE UNITED STATES: HOW CHURCHES ARE RESPONDING THROUGHOUT THE WORLD

In Canada, a unique private resettlement process allows local churches or other community organizations to sponsor refugees for resettlement above and beyond those served by the government. Private sponsorship implies both a significant financial commitment and being primarily responsible for the refugee's resettlement in that country.

Christ Community Church, a Christian Reformed congregation in Victoria, British Columbia, took up this challenge. Working with World Renew (one of about one hundred "Sponsorship Agreement

Holders" in Canada, mostly faith-based organizations that help facilitate resettlement for those sponsored privately), they welcomed
a young man from Eritrea named Ermias. Ermias, who fled a long-
standing conflict in his East African home country and escaped to
Egypt before being cleared for resettlement by the Canadian government, arrived with just two suitcases and about C $35 in his pocket.

Ermias lived with a couple from the church when he first arrived.
Despite a language barrier, Ermias has felt welcomed by the church
members, who assisted him in understanding paperwork and have
taken him hiking, biking, shopping, and even crab fishing. "Each
and every sponsorship influences the lives of both the newcomer
and church members," says Rebecca Walker, World Renew's refugee
sponsorship coordinator, noting that sponsoring a refugee was not
only an appropriate response to the biblical commands to extend
hospitality but also "an opportunity to be blessed by the incredible
friendship of newcomers from all over the world."

Similarly, in Germany, where more than one million migrants
sought refuge in 2015,[1] local churches are also responding. Our
colleague Christiane Wutschke, who leads World Relief's efforts to
empower local churches in Germany to serve asylum seekers, notes
that while the German government has assumed responsibility for
meeting basic physical needs such as shelter and food, often in large-
scale shelters, various local churches are providing friendship and
help with integrating into German society. "What's actually needed
most is at the relationship level . . . meeting German people who
care," Christiane explains.

For example, the Joshua Community (*Josua Gemeinde*)—a congregation of about 250 that is part of an evangelical movement called
Mühlheimer Verband—has offered a "Welcome to Germany" semi-
nar, translated into Arabic, Farsi, and various other languages most

common among those currently arriving in Berlin. They provide orientation to German culture and information on how basic systems like transportation, health care, and schooling work in that country. They also offer an "Intercultural Café" several days a week as an opportunity for migrants to relax and meet new friends both from the church and from various other parts of the world. Through those outreaches, many asylum seekers have become a part of the church, which now offers an Arabic language Bible study.

MINISTERING BY TEACHING ENGLISH

While welcoming newly arrived refugees presents a unique missional opportunity for local churches throughout the world, they can also meet a number of specific, ongoing needs that refugees face. One of the most significant challenges for nearly all refugees arriving in North America is the language barrier. Most refugees resettled here speak no English at all when they arrive, and only about 7 percent are fluent in English.[2] In our experience, most refugees are eager to learn. Since at least conversational English is necessary to obtain better jobs, to communicate in basic situations like shopping, banking, and going to the doctor, and to feel comfortable in their new community, this is one area where the church can effectively assist.

Faith Church, affiliated with the Evangelical Free Church of America, noticed that the demographics of their neighborhood on the north side of Indianapolis, Indiana, were changing. In particular, Steve and Joan Eisinger, who had just returned to Indianapolis after serving as missionaries in Turkey for fourteen years, learned that a small community of Meskhetian Turks lived in an apartment complex just across the street from the church.[3] The Meskhetian Turks are almost entirely Muslims. Over the past century, they have been expelled from both Georgia and Uzbekistan, then ended up in

Russia, where many viewed them as "illegal immigrants"; they were effectively stateless and faced harsh persecution from local authorities.[4] Eventually, many were resettled to the United States, and some to Indianapolis.

Steve and Joan realized that English classes would be a great way to reach that population with practical help and to share the gospel. So in 2005 Faith Church launched English language classes. They take very seriously the commitment to providing *quality* English teaching, providing intensive training for all its teachers in partnership with Wheaton College's Institute for Cross-Cultural Training. If people are not learning English, they will not come back, says Dawn Waltz, who administered the church's English program for many years.

The church also sees the classes as an opportunity to point the students to Jesus, not by preaching to them but by interacting with such kindness that they will ask their teachers about their faith. "Our philosophy is, 'Make them curious,'" Dawn says, noting that many students *do* ask questions about faith: in her first English class, four students ultimately came to faith in Christ.

The classes grew, in time, to serve refugees and other immigrants from throughout the world: at present, the classes serve nearly 200 adults and 150 children, with about 90 unpaid "staff"—mostly from Faith Church, but some from other churches as well—operating weekly classes for both adults and children. The program's mission is "to model and communicate the love of Jesus Christ to speakers of other languages through quality English teaching and personal, caring relationships."

Faith Church, which also supports a number of missionaries throughout the globe, has benefited from the missionaries' language and cultural skills as they return to Indianapolis and are uniquely equipped to minister to refugees from the same people groups they served abroad.

Faith Church has also partnered closely with other local churches. For example, just around the time that a large number of refugees from Burma began to be resettled into the Indianapolis area, a missionary who had served Burmese refugees in Thailand for many years retired and returned to his Baptist church, just up the street from Faith. The two congregations partnered: Faith provides English classes, while the Baptist church offers an after-school program for kids.

SERVING THROUGH PROVIDING LEGAL SERVICES

Another significant need for most refugees is for competent, affordable legal services. Under the law, refugees are required to apply for Lawful Permanent Resident status (the "green card") one year after arrival, which requires them to fill out a six-page application (in English), not including eight pages of instructions.

Five years after arrival, they are then generally eligible to apply to become US citizens, presuming they can prove they have been of "good moral character" throughout their residency; can pass an in-person exam in English,[5] focused on US history and government; and have not done anything else to disqualify themselves. But the application for naturalization is twenty-one pages long, not including thirteen pages of instructions. And it includes complex words like *hereditary*, *potentate*, and *heretofore*, which can be confusing to those who only recently learned English. The exam also requires a payment (in most cases) of $685. All of these issues make applying a daunting task for many who are eligible. Seeking help from a qualified attorney, though, can often cost hundreds or even thousands of dollars more.

Many well-meaning Christians have actually done significant harm to refugees and other immigrants by trying to offer legal advice without the proper training or credentials (technically, even advising someone which form to fill out to apply for an immigration benefit, such as naturalization, can be legal advice). But it *is* possible for a local church (or any other nonprofit organization) to become authorized to provide legal counsel, even if they do not have an attorney on staff, if they apply for recognition from the federal Board of Immigration Appeals (BIA), a process that involves significant training in immigration law and requires that no more than nominal fees be charged to clients. Most of our World Relief offices are BIA-recognized and have trained staff to provide legal counsel, and we also have helped empower local churches to go through the recognition process.

City Life Church, a multiethnic church affiliated with the Wesleyan Church in Grand Rapids, Michigan, is one of dozens of local churches throughout the country that have sought BIA recognition in the past several years, many of them affiliated with a multidenominational network called the Immigration Alliance. Having offered classes to help the immigrants in their community prepare for the naturalization exam for about a decade, toward the end of 2014, City Life took the next step by applying for recognition before the Board of Immigration Appeals to be able to help prepare naturalization and other immigration applications.

In order to have their BIA recognition application approved, the church sent Katie White, a recent college graduate with a passion for racial reconciliation and justice, to participate in an intensive forty-hour course on immigration law, which also included an exam. She then traveled to Indiana for on-the-job mentoring with another Wesleyan Church congregation that was already BIA-recognized and serving dozens of clients each month with legal advice. A few months after submitting the application, City Life was approved, allowing Katie to begin seeing clients.

It took several months for word to spread about the church's legal services program, but Katie now sees clients three days a week and occasionally on Saturdays. About half of those whom the church has served came to the United States as refugees, particularly from Burma, Iraq, and the Democratic Republic of the Congo, many of whom are applying to become US citizens.

In some cases, Katie notes, she has to explain the brutal limitations of US immigration law, such as when there is no legal mechanism for a resettled refugee to be reunited with an extended family member, or when an individual's travel abroad makes them ineligible for naturalization. But even then, she says, she has learned to recognize "the beauty of giving bad news," because most people are grateful just to have an honest answer amid the confusion of US immigration law, even if it is disappointing. And of course, many others do qualify to apply for their green cards or for citizenship. In its first year in operation, City Life's Immigrant Connection ministry has served approximately one hundred individuals from all over the world.

City Life aims to be a church that "offers hospitality to strangers" and that goes "to great lengths to find lost people." Providing affordable, authorized legal services has proven a unique opportunity to do both.

HELPING A REFUGEE TO BECOME A HOMEOWNER

For about eight years, I (Matthew) lived in an apartment complex where most of my neighbors were refugees. And then, quite suddenly, in 2014, the complex was sold to a new company, which raised rents dramatically and instituted new occupancy limits. My wife, daughter, and I were among many families to learn that we would not have the option to renew our lease. Saying goodbye to a community we had come to love—to our home—was painful, and a small taste of the displacement so many of our neighbors had already experienced by much more brutal forces in their home countries. It was also a reminder of a significant challenge facing many resettled refugees: finding affordable housing.

Fortunately, our forced move served as the impetus for us to go from renting an apartment to becoming homeowners. For less than the approximately $1,000 per month we had been paying in rent for a two-bedroom apartment, we could pay a monthly mortgage payment for a much larger home *and* build an asset in the process, which we may leverage one day to help send our kids to college. Now I understand intuitively why the median net worth of homeowners is thirty-six times that of the average renter[6] and why children of homeowners are 117 percent more likely to graduate from college than those whose parents rent.[7]

However, we were only able to purchase a house—and move almost overnight into a much brighter long-term financial outlook—with help from family. Most of our refugee neighbors who, like us, were covering their rent payments and surviving month-to-month but not earning enough to save up for a down payment, did not have the option to buy a house, because they arrived in the United States with no assets beyond what could fit into a suitcase. Even those who had been middle or upper class in their countries of origin had, in most cases, lost everything when they fled.

Desiree Guzman and her husband, Rick, observed this dynamic repeatedly with the various families they had befriended. Introduced to refugees through a team at their local church that partnered with World Relief's office in Aurora, Illinois, they wanted to help them break the cycle of working-class poverty so they could provide a better future for their children.

They started by inviting a family from Cuba to move into their house, directing their rent payments into a savings account so that, after about a year, the family would have enough for a down payment. Then in 2006, when Rick's younger brother, Bryan Emmanuel Guzman, died unexpectedly, the family used funds donated in Bryan's memory as the seed money for a small apartment building, allowing them to serve further families. They called the organization "Emmanuel House," as both a tribute to Bryan Emmanuel's life and as a reminder of the words of the prophet Isaiah, who foretold the coming of the Messiah who would be known as "Immanuel (which means 'God is with us')" (Isa. 7:14 NLT) and called God's people to be known as the "Repairer of Broken Walls, Restorer of Streets with Dwellings" (Isa. 58:12).

Emmanuel House now owns seven apartment units in Aurora and leases six additional properties from kingdom-minded investors. Families participating in the Emmanuel House networked savings program pay market-rate rent for eighteen months to live in an Emmanuel House property. Local churches sponsor each property, providing the financial support to cover overhead and maintenance expenses as well as financial mentoring and friendship to the family. That allows almost all of the family's rent—usually about $12,000 over eighteen months—to be saved and used as a down payment on a home at the end of the program. Already, twelve families have been able to purchase homes.

"When we come together in relationship with one another," Desiree says, "we can create the networks needed to help all our neighbors reach their full potential."

SERVING UNACCOMPANIED MINORS
AND ASYLUM SEEKERS

Local churches are also at the forefront of serving those who have fled gang violence in Central America, particularly children and youth who arrive without parents at the US-Mexico border. Under US law, such unaccompanied minors are placed in the custody of the US Department of Health and Human Services, which contracts with nonprofit organizations, many of them faith-based, to care for these children until they can be placed with a relative. Eventually, these children go before a judge who will determine if they qualify to stay lawfully or should be deported.

One location the US government has entrusted to care for these unaccompanied children is the Iglesia de Dios Pentecostal M.I. in Tampa, Florida. In the summer of 2014, as children arriving at the border made headlines, the church's senior pastor, David Rivera, received a call from a friend at the National Latino Evangelical Coalition, asking if he might consider offering part of their church facility, a sixteen-thousand-square-foot space that had been used for an after-school program, as a shelter site for unaccompanied Central American children. David hesitated at first—these children were controversial, and he did not want to face protesters. But soon he felt the conviction that caring for these children's physical, psychological, and spiritual needs was precisely what his church ought to do, so he called back and said yes.

The thousand-member Spanish-speaking congregation rallied around the opportunity, raising $80,000 in cash and in-kind donations to help renovate the space. They hired David's son, David Jr., who had been working for more than a decade in the corporate sector, to direct the center, called the *Refugio*—refuge, in Spanish—and went about the bureaucracy of getting all the necessary local, state, and federal approvals to host children in the space.

By June 2015, the facility had hosted as many as twenty-five thir-
teen- to seventeen-year-old boys at a time in eight bedrooms. The
Refugio hired youth care workers to staff the facility day and night,
teachers to provide academic support, and several clinicians to address the psychological needs of the children, each of whom had
experienced or witnessed horrific gang-related violence in El Salvador, Guatemala, or Honduras. Many also participated in optional
evangelistic and discipleship programs.

The team at the Refugio did their best to share God's love with
these vulnerable kids, who stayed with them, on average, twenty-
three days before being reunited with family members or sponsors.
Approximately 45 percent of the children were reunited with a parent
already residing in the United States, while most of the others went
to another family member and a few went to a friend of the family.

One of the most significant challenges, reports David Jr., is that
governmental policy prevents the staff of the Refugio from following up with the children once they are in the custody of their family
member or sponsor. Each will ultimately have to report to court, and
some will likely face deportation. What the church can do, though,
is to pray for the children and to be faithful to show God's love to
each as they pass through their doors.

Churches also play a critical role in caring for adult asylum seekers,
many of whom are held in detention facilities. World Relief Seattle
helps coordinate volunteers from about two dozen local churches—
most of which worship in a language other than English—to provide
culturally appropriate worship services to the individuals from all
over the world who are detained (some for just a few days, others
for months or even years) in the Northwest Detention Center in Ta-
coma, Washington. Each week, approximately five hundred detain-

ees (out of the center's maximum occupancy of 1,575 individuals) participate in one of eight weekly worship services. Last year, fifteen thousand different people participated overall, more than two thousand of whom expressed a desire to follow Christ and 266 of whom were baptized.

While most of those in detention are ultimately deported, some are granted asylum, such that World Relief Seattle can help them find employment and build a new life. While we regret that so many people are detained and that so many are forced back to their countries of origin, we are grateful to have the opportunity to express Christ's love to them for a time. At least one detainee who accepted Christ within the facility became a church planter in China after his deportation.

With more space, we could share literally hundreds of additional stories of local churches, throughout the world, that are responding with the love of Jesus to those fleeing persecution. As the world faces an unprecedented refugee crisis, though, the reality is that the need—and the opportunity—is far greater than the church's current response. Our prayer is that you and your church will join in this remarkable mission.

CHAPTER 8

HELPING WITHOUT HURTING:

UNDERSTANDING CHALLENGES TO REFUGEE ADJUSTMENT

Sameer, an Iraqi refugee, had been in the United States for two months when I (Issam) visited his home for the first time, referred by his World Relief caseworker who had noted some struggles in his adjustment. Sameer's wife, Sara, led me into their clean but sparsely furnished living room. A few minutes later, Sameer, a rail-thin thirty-three-year-old, limped into the room on a pair of crutches. I noticed that he had a scar around his neck, which he covered with a scarf. He welcomed me with a big smile and expressed his gratitude to see me, then his wife assisted him as he sat on the couch. After a short while, the air conditioner suddenly came on and gave Sameer a start. He apologized for this behavior, explaining that he is sensitive to any noise.

In sharing his story with me, Sameer said his troubles in Iraq went back to his childhood. His parents were taken regularly for questioning by Saddam Hussein's henchmen. Sameer's parents often disappeared for days and sometimes weeks before they returned home.

One day when Sameer was about six years old, his mother was taken as usual, but she never came back. At the time Sameer did not understand what had happened to her, but now he believes that she died under torture.

Because of these family dynamics, Sameer had to learn from a young age to be self-reliant. He worked hard to support himself and his siblings. He was eventually able to graduate from a community college, though he faced a number of hurdles to studying beyond high school because the government discriminated against people of his religious identity.

In 2007, when Iraq descended into a civil war between Sunni and Shiite Muslim militias, Sameer found a job as a security guard at a Baghdad hotel that catered to foreigners. One day, after finishing his shift, he was on his way home with two friends when their car was stopped at a security checkpoint. Sameer knew that he was in trouble when militants asked him and his friends to get out of the car.

Sameer had a dilemma. He carried two distinct ID cards, each with a different name implying a different sectarian identity. This was a common practice among Iraqis at the time, because people were kidnapped based on their religious affiliation, and different sectarian militias controlled different neighborhoods in Baghdad. Which ID would he present?

He handed one to the militants and held his breath. They looked it over and then grabbed Sameer and his friends, blindfolded them, and took them to a deserted place. Sameer was beaten and tortured for hours. After a lengthy and intense interrogation, he managed to successfully answer all questions concerning his religious identity, and the kidnappers decided to release him.

As they were about to let him go, one of the militants found his cellphone hidden in a bag within the car. They took his phone and called his wife. They asked her questions about the family's religion, and based on her answers, concluded that Sameer had lied to them. Sameer was severely tortured, then shot six times in different parts of his body. One of the bullets went through his neck. Believing he was dead, his kidnappers threw him into a Dumpster.

Hours later a policeman happened to pass in front of the Dumpster and noticed his body. Finding Sameer still breathing, the policeman called for an ambulance. Sameer spent the next two months in the Intensive Care Unit of a Baghdad hospital. He was in a coma for more than a month. After being discharged, Sameer and his wife decided to flee Iraq. He feared that the militia would come back to kill him. The couple escaped to Syria, where they stayed for three years before they, along with their three-year-old son, Wisam, were admitted to the United States as refugees.

As Sameer was finishing his story, Wisam burst into the living room, causing Sameer to jump in fright.

HELPING ISN'T AS EASY AS IT SEEMS

Throughout this book we have made the case enthusiastically that the arrival of refugees represents an opportunity for the church, that we have a clear biblical mandate to respond, and that refugees— rather than people to fear—are actually remarkably resilient people who are a blessing to the country that receives them.

But as Sameer's story demonstrates, working with refugees can also be *hard*.

By definition, refugees are intimately acquainted with persecution and trauma. While they can and almost always do experience healing with time, their adjustment to life in a new culture while still bearing the grief and scars—physically, psychologically, and spiritually—of what they were forced to flee is a challenging process.

For many Americans or other Westerners, even contemplating ministry to and friendship with people who have gone through such horror is intimidating. Indeed, plenty of initially enthusiastic volunteers have resigned their roles serving refugees because they became overwhelmed by the scope of the need, frustrated by the confusing behavior of their refugee friend, or hurt by miscommunication. In some cases, the refugees they had sought to help were no better off either, or may have even been harmed by the interaction.

The good news is that these dynamics are almost always avoidable. As individuals sign up to volunteer with World Relief, we recommend that they first read Steve Corbett and Brian Fikkert's superb book *When Helping Hurts: How to Alleviate Poverty without Hurting the Poor . . . and Yourself*, which outlines well how to serve the vulnerable in ways that protect their dignity—avoiding unhealthy dependency—and avert volunteer burnout.[1] World Relief staff also provide orientation and ongoing training and support for volunteers, and we encourage team ministry whenever possible, which we have found to be the most sustainable ministry model.

One of the keys to helping refugees without unintentionally hurting them or yourself is to understand both the internal challenges (particularly trauma and other mental health issues) as well as external challenges (such as adjusting to a new culture and avoiding patterns of dependency) that tend to confront those who have been forced to flee persecution and who now find themselves in a new setting.

INTERNAL CHALLENGES: TRAUMA

The term *trauma* originates from a Greek word that means "injury or wound." Psychiatrists and psychologists use the term to refer to extremely stressful, often life-threatening, events in which the survivor feels terrified, helpless, or both. Trauma is an "injury to the soul."[2] In Sameer's case, he felt terrified and helpless as he came face-to-face with death.

Researchers have found that traumatic experiences can leave psychological scars that change survivors' moods, perspectives on life, personalities, and levels of functioning.[3] One of the most common phrases that I (Issam) have heard trauma survivors repeat is, "I just want to feel like my old self again." In the aftermath of a traumatic event, memories of the ordeal take center stage and memories of other important life events fade in comparison.

> At least 39 percent of refugees experience PTSD, compared to just 1 percent of the general population.

While loss events, such as losing a loved one or struggling through a financial crisis, are painful and sad, the human body and mind experience and process trauma differently from other types of events. What distinguishes trauma from other losses is that survivors experience a consistent high level of alertness that debilitates their ability to live in a normal way.

TRAUMA AND PTSD

This psychological reaction to trauma is called "post-traumatic stress disorder" (PTSD). The concept of PTSD as a disorder started to attract medical researchers' attention after thousands of Vietnam veterans came back to the United States, displaying a number of similar psychological symptoms.[4] Women who had been raped were observed to have similar symptoms.[5]

Refugees are one of the most traumatized groups. UNHCR estimates that at least 39 percent of refugees experience PTSD, compared

to just 1 percent of the general population.[6] Other studies reveal that
the frequency and intensity of PTSD fluctuates based on the type of
traumatic exposure.[7] In particular, traumas of the sort that many (but
not all) refugees have experienced, including rape, combat exposure,
childhood neglect or physical abuse, sexual molestation, physical attack, torture, war, and kidnapping, are all associated with high rates
of PTSD. PTSD affects refugee children as well as adults, and is associated in as many as 80 percent of cases with other psychological
disorders, such as depression, substance abuse, phobias, anxiety disorders, and anger management issues.[8]

One common symptom is "intrusive thoughts,"[9] which were evi-
dent in Sameer's case. His mind uncontrollably played a videotape
of vivid details of traumatic events over and over.[10] These traumatic
memories were like a monster that followed him wherever he went,
staying with him even after he moved to the United States. All of his
attempts to get rid of scary images and sounds associated with the
trauma failed. These images and sounds came through flashbacks
during the day and nightmares during the night, which Sameer complained made it impossible for him to spend any quality time with
his family or friends. Moreover, the flashbacks made it more difficult
for him to concentrate while attending English classes, which inhib-
ited his cultural adjustment, while the terrifying nightmares left him
tired and restless.

To cope, Sameer actively avoided people, events, noises, smells,
and places that reminded him of the traumatic event, which is another common symptom of PTSD. Doctors wearing white coats reminded him of the time he spent in the hospital in Iraq, so medical
appointments were a challenge. Though he understood, on a rational
level, that the police in his new town were not out to get him, seeing
them in uniform triggered an irrational fear, such that he took side

streets to avoid driving in front of his neighborhood's police station. He had a hard time passing his driver's test because, in the Middle East, such tests are usually administered by the police, and Sameer presumed the Department of Motor Vehicle employee sitting next to him in the car was also an officer.

Avoidance symptoms also sometimes manifest themselves as a feeling of numbness. Survivors with PTSD symptoms often have difficulty experiencing a wide variety of emotions and expressing their feelings toward other people. Subsequently they may isolate themselves from others and feel less interested in engaging in activities that they used to enjoy.[11] These symptoms reflect their attempt to avoid the traumatic event, adding additional obstacles that refugees with PTSD need to overcome if they are to adjust and thrive in their new country.

Sameer often complained of an exaggerated startle response, which is also consistent with PTSD. He is startled when the air conditioner comes on, when someone knocks on the door, or when his child suddenly cries—which in turn has led to strife between him and his wife. He lives with the persistent feeling of an anticipated threat.

"I do not only remember what happened," Sameer admits, "I relive it, so I feel like I need to be on guard because it could happen again." Refugees like Sameer who have arousal symptoms may experience frequent outbursts of anger and irritability. They can have problems staying focused during a conversation. This can play havoc with interpersonal relationships and can make it difficult to maintain a job, which in turn leads to financial pressures that only add to the stress of adjustment.

Lastly, trauma survivors like Sameer often develop persistent negative and distorted beliefs and expectations about themselves and the surrounding world. Sameer often blamed *himself* for the trauma he had experienced. These irrational thoughts in return develop nega-tive trauma-related emotions, such as fear, anger, guilt, and shame, which made Sameer feel alienated from others and sense that the world is very dangerous.

UNDERSTANDING PTSD:
"HOT" VERSUS "COLD" MEMORIES

PTSD is a disorder of memory.[12] During normal times, the hu-man brain stores memories in a form that can be consciously re-called; researchers call these "cold" memories.[13] Under extreme life-threatening events, however, the human brain stores associated "hot" memories in a different format.

Cold memories are not associated with intense emotional reac-tion upon retrieval. Examples of cold memories would be general information like the name of a country's capital, or food items that you ate for breakfast. Cold memories are like a Microsoft Word file that you intentionally open to recall information. In contrast, hot memories are like a pop-up YouTube ad that can appear at any mo-ment, capturing your attention with images and sounds.

Cold memories are usually stored in an organized manner with a clear chronological order because they are typically stored with the assistance of the hippocampus, a part of the brain widely believed to add chronological order to events.[14] Hot memories are typically stored with the assistance of the amygdala, the part of the brain that serves as a radar, detecting threats and preparing the body to re-act accordingly. While cold memories are saved in a narrative form, hot memories are fragmented and stored in the form of sensory ele-ments—images, smells, voices, thoughts, feelings, and physiological responses.[15]

Hot memories are associated with intense feelings of horror and helplessness, as if the trauma were recurring in the present. Once these memories are triggered, survivors such as Sameer can experience a full-blown panic attack with symptoms that include increased heartrate, fast breathing, and high blood pressure. Since these memories can occur anytime, trauma survivors learn quickly to avoid any potential cues—images, places, noises, thoughts, feelings and such—that remind them of the event.

These triggers, which induce an intense emotional reaction similar to the one experienced in past traumas, form what is known as a "fear cascade."[16] The fear cascade looks like a web of triggers made up of sensory elements (images, voices, smells, etc.), thoughts, feelings, and physiological responses (racing heart, rapid breathing).

The Fear Cascade

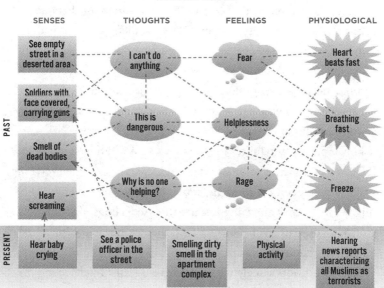

In the case of Sameer, one trigger—or a combination of two or more—can induce an acute psychological response similar to the one he experienced in Iraq. In many ways this fear complex is similar to walking through a minefield: one seemingly minor trigger (such as hearing a baby's cry) can lead to another, and ultimately to a full-blown panic attack where the survivor believes he is about to die. One day Sameer had a panic attack after walking downstairs from his apartment. He got tired so he sat down. As he was resting, he felt his heart pound (a physiological trigger). That triggered the memory, which led to feeling helpless and believing that he would die. His physiological response became similar to the one he had experienced during the initial trauma. If not treated, PTSD can become debilitating, as Sameer's experience illustrates.

FINDING HEALING

Fortunately, though, PTSD *is* treatable: a variety of therapies—primarily focused on psychotherapy, but sometimes with medication to decrease the frequency and intensity of physiological symptoms, such as nightmares and insomnia—have been effective.[17] A combination of therapy and psychotropic medications can decrease the symptoms' frequency and intensity, and can help a survivor gain control over his or her life.

However, many refugees do not have a good understanding of PTSD as a disorder that can be treated. Depending on their level of education and culture of origin, some refugees experiencing PTSD might believe they are going insane. Intense feelings of shame and guilt may prevent them from sharing their symptoms with others outside their household.

Those who work closely with refugees can assist by detecting the PTSD symptoms we have described. When symptoms become apparent—and when refugees are willing—those seeking to assist refugees can encourage them to seek professional help. Just as for many non-refugees, there can be a sense of stigma attached to asking for assistance with a mental health problem, so it may be helpful to share about a time that you (or a family member or friend) sought counseling when facing a challenging situation.

Professional help may be available from a number of sources. Some refugee resettlement agencies offer counseling services with a particular cultural sensitivity to the needs of refugees; ethnic-specific community groups may offer similar services in some locations. A physician may also be able to help, or to make a referral to a psychiatrist with more expertise.

The reality is, though, that access to mental health care is not as accessible as we believe that it should be—either for refugees or the general population. Christ followers can address this need as well: those with financial resources could support affordable, culturally sensitive counseling. Mental health professionals can offer their services on a volunteer basis. We can all advocate for public policies to prioritize adequate access to services.

It is also important to note for volunteers and others who interact intensively with refugees that listening to traumatic stories can induce traumatic symptoms in the *listener*. Psychologists refer to this phenomenon as "vicarious traumatization."[18] Volunteers or workers who spend time with refugees and listen to their stories might start to experience flashbacks, nightmares, and lapses in their memories about a trauma story that they have heard. It is important for individuals who work with refugees to be consistently self-aware when these symptoms appear, take time off to disconnect, recharge spiritually and emotionally, and seek professional help if the symptoms persist.

Trauma is a reality impacting many refugees, so if we want to serve well and not be hurt ourselves, we need to understand it. But it is not an insurmountable barrier: God made human beings to be remarkably resilient, and we see that as we witness refugees experience healing and overcome the traumas of their past.

EXTERNAL CHALLENGES: CULTURAL ADJUSTMENT

While many refugees, like Sameer, face internal challenges as a result of the trauma they have previously experienced, they must also deal with a number of *external* challenges as they adjust to a new and often dramatically different culture. To serve refugees well, we must also understand how culture impacts their adjustment process.

Culture is defined as the "learned meaning system that consists of patterns of traditions, beliefs and values, and norms that pass from one generation to another."[19] We each are taught from a young age to follow certain cultural principles, which are usually reinforced by parents, teachers, religious leaders, and other authority figures. These cultural principles influence patterns of communication, regulate daily activities, and guide and govern relationships. When refugees relocate and start to encounter people from the hosting culture, they discover that other cultures have different rules and regulations, which can produce interpersonal tension and conflict.

CULTURE AS AN ICEBERG

Culture has some aspects that are observable, but most can only be suspected, imagined, or intuited. Viewing culture as an iceberg provides a helpful analogy. Like an iceberg, the visible part of culture makes up only a small portion of a much larger whole. The invisible piece of the culture includes beliefs, values, traditions, and thought patterns, while the visible part includes clothes, food, music, and language.[20]

Culture as an Iceberg

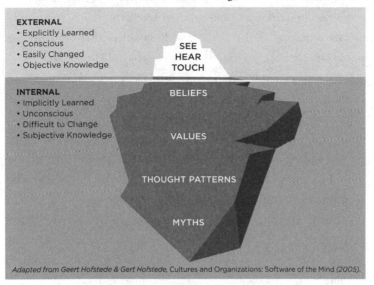

Adapted from Geert Hofstede & Gert Hofstede, Cultures and Organizations: Software of the Mind (2005).

In the early stages of cross-cultural interactions, people tend to note the similarities between the new culture and their own, since they initially experience and observe the visible part of the other culture.[21] As time passes, though, cross-cultural interactions can become increasingly emotionally charged as parties begin to perceive and interpret various incidents quite differently, as the invisible dynamics of culture shape perception.

INDIVIDUAL-ORIENTED VERSUS
COMMUNITY-ORIENTED CULTURES

Anthropologist Geert Hofstede classified contemporary societies into two general categories: community-oriented cultures and individual-oriented cultures.[22] In community-oriented cultures, which are the norm in Asia, the Middle East, Africa, and Latin America (the regions from which most of the world's refugees come), children are raised to think as *we* instead of *I*, and are encouraged to value traits that promote group cohesiveness and harmony, such as loyalty, hierarchy, respect of the elders, and hospitality. They are taught to put the interest of the group in front of their individual interests.

On the other hand, members of individual-oriented cultures (particularly in northern Europe and North America) are raised to develop traits such as independence, assertiveness, being task-oriented, and being time-efficient. Activities and decisions are geared to preserving and enhancing the individual's interests first. The ultimate goal of parenting within individual-oriented culture is to rear children who can handle life's challenges on their own.

It is natural—but also problematic, particularly from a Christian perspective—to fall into ethnocentrism, which is defined as "seeing one's own group . . . as virtuous and superior, one's own standards of value as universal, and out-groups as contemptible and inferior."[23] One of the central conflicts in the book of Acts was between those who believed that Gentiles who wanted to follow Jesus needed to adapt to the Jewish culture they viewed as superior and those—led by Paul, who reiterated the point repeatedly in his letters to the churches—who insisted that God does not discriminate between cultures, and neither should we (Acts 15:8–9). However, while it is unhelpful to view one culture as *better* than another, it *is* important to recognize how they are *different*.

One way to appreciate the value of different cultures is to view them from a pragmatic perspective. Author Fons Trompenaars suggests that culture is the result of finding solutions to problems with the environment, time, and relationships with others.[24] Cultural principles and practices that might "work" in some societies may not work in others. If refugees or those who interact with them do not come to realize quickly the existence of cultural differences in norms and expectations, conflicts might arise. Refugees in particular need to be equipped to resolve cultural misunderstandings with their employers, resettlement agencies, or volunteers *before* these conflicts add additional obstacles that hinder their abilities to become self-sufficient. In Sameer's case, it was important for him to learn to communicate and resolve conflict differently so that he could avoid being mistakenly perceived as a passive-aggressive or hostile person.

CULTURE, COMMUNICATION, AND CONFLICT-RESOLUTION STYLES

Each culture has preferred styles of communication and conflict resolution. When resolving a conflict, most people in an individual-oriented culture like North America prefer a direct "discussion style" of communication.[25] Because they place a high value on time, they prefer to communicate directly using short sentences rather than value-laden parables and stories. Emotional interjections are viewed as disruptive and inappropriate. Those in individual-oriented cultures tend to believe that the parties involved in the conflict should engage together directly, without involving an intermediary or a third party to resolve the conflict.

On the other hand, refugee groups who mainly come from community-oriented cultures usually prefer an indirect approach to conflict resolution. The two most common conflict-resolution styles among refugees are an "accommodation" style, which is common among refugees from many parts of Asia, and the "dynamic" style, which is common among those from the Middle East.[26] Both styles emphasize the importance of using intermediaries in resolving misunderstanding so that the conflict can be kept under complete control and the risk of anyone's feelings being hurt is minimized.

One reason members of these cultures prefer an indirect style emerges from a cultural value known as "saving face." These cultures believe that every effort should be made to avoid a situation where someone is publicly embarrassed.

Consider the following phone conversation between Sameer and Steve (his American work supervisor):

> Steve: We really have to complete the order by the assigned deadline. So I need you to work on Sunday this week.
> Sameer: [*pauses*] I see. Sunday is a very special day for me. It is my son Wisam's birthday.
> Steve: That's wonderful. I hope it's a very special day.
> Sameer: Thank you, sir.

Steve, a Western man, left this conversation believing that Sameer would show up to work on Sunday, while Sameer presumed that Steve understood the reason why he would *not*. Such differences in conflict resolution and communication styles can lead to confusion and misunderstanding between refugees and those with whom they interact.

THE JOURNEY TO CULTURAL ADJUSTMENT

All resettled refugees are grateful to escape danger and move to a safe country, but their journey to cultural adjustment is never immediate and rarely smooth. Resettled refugees generally pass through a roller-coaster-like four-phase adjustment process: *honeymoon, cultural shock, adjustment,* and *mastery.*[27]

In the *honeymoon* stage, refugees feel life is wonderful and things make sense. Family members finally enjoy having time with one another in a safe place. During this stage, refugees are usually overwhelmed with the help and compassion that they receive from volunteers and the community. Shopping is fascinating, food is available, and streets are clean.

A few months later, reality starts to sink in. Learning English turns out to be difficult. Professional skills or educational degrees do not transfer to the new country. The only available jobs are entry-level positions that are physically exhausting. The health-care system is confusing and difficult to access. Rent and other bills are overwhelming. The list goes on. At this *culture shock* phase, refugees realize that life is harder than what they had expected. Some feel homesick, and even question their decision to relocate to the resettlement country; some may feel like giving up.

In time, though, refugees gain some level of normalcy. They start to read social cues, gain confidence in communicating in English, and start to laugh at their own mistakes. This is the *adjustment* phase. It involves developing realistic expectations.

The final *mastery* phase is marked by learning skills that allow the refugee to start believing in his or her own abilities. It involves the capacity to exercise some measure of control over life. Refugees feel that they are *home*. They begin to appreciate and incorporate many aspects of the hosting culture.

Not all refugees pass through each of these four stages, nor do they move through them at the same pace. To best assist and come alongside refugees during their adjustment journey, it is important to understand that it is an emotional process and that different refugees have different learning curves, often marked with both setbacks and breakthroughs.

REFUGEE FAMILY DYNAMICS

Adjustment does not only take place on an individual level. Refugee families need to go through the process of adjustment as a unit.

Under normal circumstances, there is a hierarchy within the family, with the parents (and, in many cultures, particularly the father) at the top of this hierarchy as the family faces decisions and disciplines children as needed.

When a refugee family is resettled, children and adolescents who are immersed in school and more exposed to mainstream culture typically learn the language and acculturate faster than their parents. With faster adjustment, children and adolescents acquire more power within the family structure, as parents become increasingly dependent on them. Refugee parents have occasionally said that they no longer dare to discipline their children, fearing that they might need their help later to translate a bill or respond to an important call. Psychologists refer to this phenomenon as "role reversal."[28] This dynamic can be very challenging for many refugee families, particularly because they typically come from cultures where family roles are clearly defined and children are expected not to question the authority of their parents.

Marriages can also be strained by the stress of cultural adjustment, particularly when a couple comes from a culture where views of gender roles are different from those in mainstream American culture. In many cultures, for example, women do not generally work outside the house. In the United States, most women do, and in fact may need to because of financial pressures, since it is difficult for a family to be financially self-sufficient on a single minimum-wage income.

While some of these family dynamics simply take adjustment time to address effectively, we can help refugees by providing counseling and orientation and by explaining how the host culture views these family issues. Teachers, volunteers, and others who influence children can encourage them to respect their parents *and* their parents' culture.

HEALING THROUGH RELATIONSHIPS

Refugees face a long journey to adjust and thrive in their new resettlement country. Many have been abused, betrayed, and mistreated prior to arrival, and some may have difficulty trusting others, as they expect to be hurt again. The deepest wounds that any individual carries are relational in nature, and refugees are no exception. As a psychotherapist, I (Issam) believe that relational wounds can be healed only by relational remedies through developing healthy relationships with God and others.

In my opinion, there is no better healing experience for a refugee family than getting to know an American family that chooses to come alongside them and guide them through their new journey. When refugees are treated with love, patience, respect, and honor instead of rejection, intolerance, shame, and disgrace, past wounds heal and refugees learn to expect to be treated with kindness and dignity again.[29]

By the same token, an American volunteer who breaks promises or abuses the refugee's confidence can actually significantly set back a refugee's adjustment by reinforcing the expectation that people cannot be trusted. Through new healthy relationships, refugees learn to trust others again and develop a sense of the world as a safe place. They also come to learn their own values as individuals.

PATERNALISM AND AVOIDING DEPENDENCY AMONG REFUGEES

One key final point—if we want to help without hurting—is to keep in mind that the ultimate goal is for refugees to become self-sufficient, able to meet all their basic needs without external assistance. Although not all reach this stage, because of issues related to medical conditions and age (just like some Americans), the overwhelming majority have the capacity to do so. Therefore, volunteers and resettlement agency staff need to periodically examine their relationships with refugees whom they are assisting to make sure that these individuals do not become codependent on them but rather develop the skills they need to function independently in their new home. Volunteers must gradually transition from being "helpers" to simply being friends, in a reciprocal relationship.

Volunteers and others who serve displaced people also need to avoid falling into the trap of becoming paternalistic. This typically occurs when a volunteer or service provider makes decisions that refugees can make on their own. Those who fall into a paternalistic mode might be motivated by the belief that the refugees will be better off or less vulnerable to harm if they make decisions on their behalf. While it is good to keep in mind that vulnerable individuals may need protection, refugees usually adjust in a more timely and healthy manner if allowed and encouraged to make their own decisions.

FROM REFUGEE TO MENTOR

Resettled refugees have a long journey to full adjustment. Fortunately, most of them are resilient. With the right guidance and direction, refugees can succeed well in their new resettling country. Volunteers, churches, and others in the communities who receive them can play an integral role, helping—rather than unintentionally inflicting further harm—if they understand the unique challenges these new residents confront.

For Sameer and his family, the journey has been difficult, with multiple setbacks along the way, but their case is also a model of how, with time and with appropriate help from a receiving community, refugees can ultimately thrive. Sameer's traumatic symptoms diminished significantly with therapy. He received the medical care he needed and no longer requires crutches to walk. He and his wife have a new baby, and Wisam is adjusting well to school. After several years of language classes, both Sameer and his wife now feel comfortable speaking English.

Two years ago, Sameer quit his job and started to drive his own cab. Today he owns three taxis, which he hires more recently arrived refugees to drive. He also recently began evening classes in computer science at a local community college, and he has helped us at World Relief by sharing his story at public events. Though Sameer needed help and healing when he first arrived, and continues to experience some symptoms of PTSD, he is glad that he can now help others. When a welcoming community understands the unique challenges to adjustment that refugees face, they can help them to thrive.

CHAPTER 9

ROOT CAUSES:

RESPONDING TO THE LARGER ISSUES
THAT COMPEL PEOPLE TO FLEE

When we welcome refugees to our communities, we follow God's command to welcome the stranger and love our neighbor. While Western media attention about the refugee crisis tends to focus on those being resettled into the United States or Canada or seeking asylum in Europe, in reality only a small percentage of today's estimated sixty million forcibly displaced people will *ever* reach communities in the West. The vast majority remain in the Middle East, Africa, and Asia.[1] The church's response to the global refugee crisis must also include and prioritize supporting local churches and relief efforts in the countries most impacted.

But to fully love our neighbor, we must also grapple with *why* people are displaced in the first place. As we welcome refugees and learn from them the horrific realities that compelled them to leave their homelands, naturally we will want to do all we can to prevent similar persecution from recurring elsewhere and turning more people into refugees. Envisioning a world where mothers, children, and families are safe from the dangers associated with displacement requires us to look more deeply at its root causes. Why do people flee their homes?

How can we stem the tide of displacement? How can the church respond most effectively? Asking deeper questions not only informs how we react to the urgent needs during and after a crisis but also helps us consider how to prevent more displacement.

ASKING WHY

We often think of war, genocide, or natural disasters as the causes of crisis migration, but often there are deeper reasons.[2] Political or natural disasters may trigger the mass movement of people, but underlying structural factors provide the context for these triggers and often serve as their impetus.[3] These stressors lead to the tipping points we so often see in the news. Years of entrenched poverty, unjust government policy, or environmental issues may actually be the root causes.

Asking *why* is helpful for discovering the fundamental problems that need to be addressed. In 2010, the trigger that resulted in large-scale death, destruction, and migration in Haiti was an earthquake. But why did so many people die—at least 120,000,[4] by the most conservative estimates, and perhaps as many as 316,000[5]—compared to other similar earthquakes? An earthquake of the same magnitude (7.1 on the Richter scale) hit near Anchorage, Alaska, on January 24, 2016, but you likely did not even hear about it, because no lives were lost and just four homes were damaged—incomparably less damage than in Haiti.[6] *Why?* For one, many concrete structures in Port au Prince were not properly reinforced; construction did not meet Haiti's building codes. *But why were they not reinforced?* In many cases, because contractors cheated on their materials to boost their profits.

Corruption, then, is one root cause of the 2010 Haitian humanitarian and migration crisis triggered by an earthquake. If we dig a little deeper, we learn that, not surprisingly, vulnerable people were taken advantage of more often than others, which leads to another underlying issue, namely, injustice against marginalized communities.

Similarly, war and conflict are the immediate cause behind the flight of most of the world's refugees. In recent years, Syria, Iraq, the Democratic Republic of the Congo, South Sudan, Somalia, Afghanistan, and Ukraine, among others, have experienced mass displacement as a result of war. If we look deeper, though, we find that conflict generally emerges because of persistent oppression, entrenched poverty, despotism, corruption, or other root causes.[7]

A STORY OF TRANSFORMATION

If we keep digging deeper, we find that these vulnerabilities are rooted in particular values, beliefs, and worldviews—each of which, as Christians, we believe can be changed, which can lead to better outcomes. At World Relief, we use the metaphor of a tree to imagine how these realities can ultimately be transformed.

If we want to address the effects of forced migration, poverty, and conflict, we must look at the *values* that cause political and social tension, including the societal values that influence behavior. How does a society think about ethnicity, women, and children, for example? Far too often we hear stories where certain groups are overlooked, exploited, or oppressed merely because of their race, gender, age, or faith.

But what informs a society's morals? Its worldview, the "assumptions and frameworks people make about the nature of reality,"[8] as anthropologist Paul Hiebert explains, shapes them. Often referred to simply as "beliefs," worldview is composed of thoughts—both conscious and unconscious as informed by emotions and feelings—that

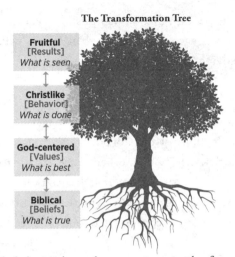

The Transformation Tree

Fruitful
[Results]
What is seen

Christlike
[Behavior]
What is done

God-centered
[Values]
What is best

Biblical
[Beliefs]
What is true

are handed down through generations in the form of culture and traditions. They include assumptions, ideas about the existence of God, whether God is good or capricious, and our purpose for living.

What people believe and value matter because they drive their *behaviors*, whether good or bad. As we think about how we can most effectively bring positive change to any culture, including our own, we must understand the relationship between behaviors, values, and beliefs. Change that yields results without a corresponding change in values and beliefs will be superficial and often temporary. Root causes that trigger a crisis may remain long after the crisis has dissipated, leaving people, groups, and even whole nations susceptible to future humanitarian crises.

The story of our colleague Samedy Sok illustrates how a dangerous belief system bore the fruit of death and displacement, but also the hope for transformation that is possible.

Samedy was a teenager in 1975, when Communist dictator Pol Pot came to power in Cambodia. In order to achieve Pol Pot's vision of a classless "agricultural communism"—rooted in an atheistic belief system without regard for human life—the Khmer Rouge guerilla movement he led isolated Cambodia from the rest of the world. The regime confiscated all private property, banned religion, eliminated currency, and forced hundreds of thousands of people—including Samedy and his family—from urban areas to rural labor camps. Many died along the way. Many more died of starvation in the following years, as the social engineering led to famine. Many others, especially those (like Samedy's family) viewed as "intellectuals," were executed and placed in mass graves. In just four years, from 1975 to 1979, an estimated 1.7 million Cambodians lost their lives in one of the most horrific genocides of the twentieth century.[9]

After being forced to leave their home at gunpoint in 1975, a year later Samedy's family was separated from one another. Within a few years, Samedy's mother, two sisters, and brother were all executed. He cared for two of his three remaining sisters, but then they were separated again.

Samedy was thrown into prison where he was kept shackled. Though not a Christian at that time, Samedy prayed each night for the chance to see the sun again, because the night was when prisoners would be taken for execution. One night, he says, he saw a vision of Jesus in a white robe, telling him to have hope, because he would survive (when Samedy told this to his cellmate the next morning, the cellmate told him he had been hallucinating).

In 1979, when Vietnam invaded Cambodia, Samedy was released from prison. He returned to his hometown to find his family but, not locating them, he traveled from camp to camp within Cambodia, asking if anyone had news of or had seen his family. No one had. He then continued to the border with Thailand, where he became a refugee. After a short time in the camp, he volunteered to work with UNHCR, registering other refugees. One day, a thin, frail man came to be registered. His appearance was so distorted by years of famine and abuse that Samedy did not immediately recognize his own father. Samedy was overjoyed to be reunited and discover that his three remaining sisters were also still alive.

It is not difficult to see how Pol Pot and the Khmer Rouge's worldview led to particular behaviors (labor camps, imprisonment, and executions), which resulted in devastating fruit for an entire country. However, Samedy's story also demonstrates how a positive belief system can lead to transformation: in the Khao-I-Dang refugee camp in Thailand, Samedy became a Christian. After resettling to the United States in 1982 and being welcomed by a Lutheran church in Philadelphia, Samedy's newfound faith and his own experience inspired him to welcome and serve other refugees, first with an affiliate of the Lutheran Immigration and Refugee Service and later as the director of World Relief's office in Anne Arundel, Maryland. A relationship with Jesus transformed Samedy's life, and that new foundation influenced his actions, which in turn have borne fruit in many others' lives.

Obviously, most of us are not in a position to take out a dictator, but all of us—both in our own communities and by partnering with churches elsewhere in the world—can seek to promote a worldview guided by the values of Jesus, beginning in our own lives. We can seek peace, practice forgiveness, extend hospitality, and pursue justice. Samedy's story is a testimony to the long-term effects that are possible when we allow these values to shape our lives and our communities.

THE SPIRAL OF INJUSTICE

As we seek to bring transformation into situations of vulnerability, we have to understand the effects of injustice. Crisis migration, pervasive poverty, social strife, and political oppression can have a devastating effect on human self-worth and dignity. Marginalized people often define vulnerability in social and psychological terms, mentioning shame, inferiority, powerlessness, humiliation, fear, and hopelessness.[10] In the words of a woman from Moldova, vulnerability "is pain; it feels like a disease. . . . It eats away one's dignity and drives one into total despair."[11]

In its worst form, the psychological impact associated with displacement can strip people from their sense of human dignity. Such negative impact can cause them to believe they have been cut off from God's love or even forsaken by God altogether. According to author Bryant Myers, "A lifetime of suffering, deception, and exclusion is internalized in ways that result in [people] no longer knowing who they truly are or why they were created."[12]

At its worst, injustice is complex and multilayered. For the vulnerable, a myriad of factors—disease, hunger, poverty, violence—work together to create a downward spiral that leaves people feeling profoundly helpless. Many times this downward spiral of violence and poverty is at work well before a family leaves their home, whether because of a trigger or tipping point. Sometimes the risks associated with escape are perceived to be less than the risks of staying.

Once they've chosen to leave home, however, the displaced are often subject to risks they didn't anticipate. Migration exposes them to new forms of violence or poverty. One in six Syrians who have escaped to Lebanon, for example, live in extreme poverty.[13]

Refugees are also disproportionately vulnerable to human trafficking, as opportunistic criminals prey upon refugees to conscript men, women, and children into forced labor, sexual slavery, or soldiering.

Refugees and others displaced by conflict—especially women and girls—are particularly vulnerable to sexual violence. Rape is a weapon of war in the Democratic Republic of the Congo, where incidents of rape are reportedly the highest in the world, with nearly fifty women raped every *hour*.[14] Rebel soldiers refer to rape as "cheaper than bullets."[15] One sixteen-year-old boy, who was a soldier for two years, said, "If we see girls, it's our right . . . we can violate them."[16]

"Survival sex," where women and children are forced to exchange sex for basic services such as shelter, food, or protection, is also sadly common in humanitarian crises. Sometimes government troops or international agencies—the very people who are supposed to protect them—exploit refugees. As authors Nicholas Kristof and Sheryl WuDunn note, this horrific problem is made even worse because some cultures stigmatize women and girls who have been raped or sexually violated, leaving them "socially isolated, shunned, or even subject to further acts of violence from family or community members intent on protecting a traditional sense of honor."[17]

This dynamic, where migration, violence, and poverty converge, leaves people on a downward spiral of injustice. Our response must tackle both the causes and consequences of this spiral. The church, driven by a biblical call to justice, has a key role to play.

A BIBLICAL RESPONSE

A biblical vision of justice is anchored deeply in the person and sacrificial love of Jesus and is inseparable from the essence of the gospel itself. In the Bible, we encounter a God who loves justice, demands justice, and executes it for the needy (Ps. 33:5; Mic. 6:8; Zech. 7:9). Most important, the biblical mandate doesn't simply refer to injustice, it provides a pathway for stopping and reversing the spiral of injustice.

Two words are used for *justice* in the Old Testament. The first, *mishpat*, means "rendering judgment," or "giving people what they are due," and is sometimes referred to as "rectifying justice." The second word, *tsedeqa*, means "the right thing," or especially, "right relationships," and is referred to as "primary justice." These words are often paired in Scripture as "justice and righteousness."

Taken together, *mishpat* and *tsedeqa* present a relational definition of justice, an important dimension that has too often been overlooked. They capture both God's action, when referring to the covenant between God and His people, and also His followers' conduct, when referring to social relationships. This should not surprise us given the centrality of love in the Old and New Testaments: for example, "Love the LORD your God with all your heart and with all your soul and with all your strength" (Deut. 6:5, echoed in Matt. 22:37), and "Love your neighbor as yourself" (Lev. 19:18; Matt. 22:39). This relational aspect is a pivotal dimension of justice.[18]

In its fullness, justice is about right relationships—relationships that work. Injustice is about relationships that don't. Justice for those whom philosopher Nicholas Wolterstorff terms "the quartet of the vulnerable"[19]—the orphan, widow, immigrant (including the refugee), and poor—is especially important to God.[20] Injustice occurs when these people are left out, oppressed, or exploited. Justice occurs when they are included.

War, oppression, and hunger are usually symptoms of broken relationships. Relationships that have gone awry, have been ignored for too long, or are downright harmful—whether between people, villages, governments, and even the West and the Global South—lead to suffering, and sometimes deeply entrenched patterns of evil as well.

When we approach the problems of suffering as relational, our response changes, sometimes profoundly. Instead of just giving charity or aid, we must seek to strengthen relationships within a community, including especially the relationship of the vulnerable to the powerful, the local church to all ethnicities, and even the citizens to its government. While we may pursue our goals out of hearts of sympathy, the better way is through biblical justice. Only through loving and honorable relationships can sustainable change be ultimately won, affecting the root causes that have compelled so many to flee their homes throughout the world today.

When we live out justice in our relationships, we give witness to the person of Jesus and effect change. Neighbor to neighbor. Tribe to tribe. The poor to the wealthy. The wealthy to the poor. Governments to their citizens. God to His people and His people to creation. These relationships, when stitched together justly, weave a tapestry of hope that can fundamentally change society for the better. When local churches *here* work alongside churches on the front lines of the most horrific instances of injustices, sharing resources and ideas, this can make a profound difference.

For example, a few years ago, a pastor from Indiana partnered with Marcel, his pastor friend from the Democratic Republic of the Congo, to explore how to tackle the root causes of conflict in a country plagued by injustice for decades. They convened local pastors for a retreat where they forgave one another for not working to bring peace between their congregations and communities. They vowed to do something different—*together.*

Over several months, the pastors worked within their churches to form "Village Peace Committees" to address community conflicts. Too often, interpersonal strife at the local level had escalated into vengeful cycles of violence, some of which ultimately forced people to flee. By helping the local church to wage peace, many conflicts have been resolved *before* they could spiral into violence.

While always right, prioritizing relationships can be costly. When Pastor Ephraim from Jordan decided to open his church to Syrian refugee children and their mothers, many from his Jordanian congregation left for good. Kids from the community taunted Syrian children as they walked to the church to learn life skills and participate in activities to overcome their trauma. Now Ephraim recounts how his church has changed for the better. "The message of Jesus is to love our enemies," he told his people. What he didn't expect, given the initial hostility, was for members of his congregation to eventually become friends with Syrians.

Reframing the fundamental conundrums in the world as *relational* rather than only as problems requiring aid, funding, or programs doesn't take away the need for professional, and often technical, expertise. It also does not eliminate the need for resources: indeed, Pastor Ephraim is able to provide this safe place for Syrian refugee children in his church in significant part thanks to the financial support of people halfway across the world who have given sacrificially to World Relief's work training and equipping local churches like Ephraim's to provide quality service.

> The Bible challenges us to persevere—in welcoming refugees in our own communities but also in the larger tasks of addressing the root injustices that compel them to flee.

By bringing together both best practices and an emphasis on restoring relationships according to a biblical view of justice, we begin to see permanent changes in people and communities—changes that have the power to transform whole societies, and change us, too, along the way.

TRANSFORMATION IS POSSIBLE

The complex, violent realities that refugees flee are evidence of horrific evil in our world, but their stories also remind us that transformation, healing, and justice *are* possible.[21] The Bible challenges us to persevere—in welcoming refugees in our own communities but also in the larger tasks of addressing the root injustices that compel them to flee—with the promise that "at the proper time we will reap a harvest if we do not give up" (Gal. 6:9).

Samedy's story is a remarkable example. In 2015, after serving refugees in the United States for decades, Samedy and his wife, Sovannarorth, felt that God was calling them to return to Cambodia, where Samedy now directs World Relief's office there. Though only about 2 percent of Cambodians are Christian,[22] Samedy and his colleagues work with a network of about six hundred small cell churches to run child development and hygiene programs, teach teenagers biblical practices to help stop the spread of HIV/AIDS, provide education to communities at risk of human trafficking, and offer training on agriculture and savings groups to help parents feed their families well and generate income for school fees, medications, or unanticipated expenses. As they meet tangible needs, they also have the opportunity to point people to Jesus, growing the local church and instilling the beliefs and values that, Samedy prays, will prevent his country from ever revisiting the horrific violence that claimed the lives of most of his family nearly forty years ago.

The global refugee crisis is indeed global. It isn't a question of

> It isn't a question of whether we should respond here (in the West) or there (at the crises' points of origin), nor if we should address immediate needs or root causes. We can and must do all of the above.

whether we should respond here (in the West) or there (at the crises' points of origin), nor if we should address immediate needs or root causes. We can and must do all of the above. It takes the church in every part of the world—from Cambodia to the United States, the Congo to Canada, Germany to Jordan, and everywhere in between—working together to address the crisis. How we respond now could define the church—and the world—for a generation or more.

CHAPTER 10

CONFRONTING INJUSTICE:

WHY POLICY MATTERS

In May 1939, as the Nazi government had begun to confiscate Jewish properties and burn synagogues, more than nine hundred German Jews fled the country on the SS St. Louis bound for Cuba, with the ultimate goal of reaching refuge in the United States. Before they arrived in Cuba, though, most of their visas were revoked. When the ship turned north to Miami, they were not allowed to dock in the United States either, despite direct appeals to President Franklin Roosevelt. The ship returned to Europe. While some were able to reach safety in the United Kingdom, 254 of the St. Louis's passengers were forced back to continental Europe and were eventually killed in the Holocaust.[1]

The same year, a bipartisan bill in Congress to allow in twenty thousand Jewish refugee children from Germany was introduced. Laura Delano Houghteling, wife of the US Commissioner of Immigration, fretted that "20,000 charming children would all too soon grow up into 20,000 ugly adults," reflecting the sentiment of many Americans at the time. Her cousin, President Roosevelt, did not support the bill, which ultimately was defeated.[2] In 1941, the Roosevelt administration tightened restrictions on Jewish refugees, worried that some could be—or could become—Nazi spies.[3]

This history is personal to me (Stephan). Recently I found my wife, Belinda, staring at a photo of her grandfather, Alexis Koshanov, or "Grandpa Alex," as Belinda knew him. Alexis fled Lithuania before Hitler's anti-Semitic whisper campaign, but was turned away at Ellis Island because he was Jewish. He later immigrated into the United States via Canada, but his sister died in Auschwitz and his brother barely survived Dachau. "I am a refugee, just two generations removed," Belinda said, tears filling her eyes.

These stories are an important illustration of why refugee policy matters: the decisions of elected officials directly impact people made by God, whose lives we believe are precious. They also dictate whether churches will continue to have the opportunity to serve refugees in any particular community.

POLICY IS ABOUT PEOPLE

While the majority of our work with World Relief to empower local churches to serve vulnerable refugees involves directly, relationally ministering to human needs, we cannot holistically love our neighbors without engaging questions of policy that ultimately impact people.

As Noel Castellanos, CEO of the Christian Community Development Association, notes, an appropriate biblical response to the vulnerable means to act with compassion to those in need, such as providing a furnished apartment for newly arrived refugees and making sure they have enough to eat during the first weeks of arrival, when they have no income of their own. However, it also requires us to help equip them to develop the gifts God has given them, securing employment, and working to restore and develop the community around them. If we truly love people, we will certainly look for opportunities to proclaim the hope of the gospel, because we believe that nothing is more transformative than a personal relationship with Jesus. But truly loving our neighbors also requires another component: to confront the injustices that keep the vulnerable from flourishing as God intends.[4]

Public policies directly impact both whether refugees will be allowed to resettle and how successful they will be at integrating once they arrive. For example, most refugees in the United States rely on food stamps for their first few months, at least until they can secure employment. Therefore, cuts to food stamp programs directly impact many refugee families. Federal and state funding decisions also impact a refugee resettlement agency's ability to help provide initial housing and a caseworker to help orient new arrivals.

In the United States, we take for granted that those admitted as refugees are authorized to work, which allows most to become self-sufficient. But granting employment authorization is also a policy decision: in some countries, refugees are *not* eligible to work and are thus denied the dignity of providing for themselves (at least, legally), a reality some categories of immigrants in the United States also face.

Religious liberty provisions are a matter of policy as well: the First Amendment of the US Constitution protects the rights of all residents—whether citizens or not—both to share their faith with others and to choose to believe or not believe, without coercion. But such liberties are not universally recognized: many countries enforce brutal restrictions on voluntary religious conversion.

Policies can even facilitate or block the ability of local churches to minister to refugees. After all, if refugee resettlement is halted altogether—as one recent bill in the US House of Representatives proposed—the remarkable missional opportunities we have described throughout this book will cease to exist, at least in this country.[5] A major limiting factor on the scope of Christian ministry to refugees in any given country is the ceiling of refugee admissions that the national government sets.

A BIBLICAL BASIS FOR ADVOCACY

Advocating before the governmental entities with the authority to change policies is an essential element of loving our neighbors (see Luke 10:27). Dr. Martin Luther King Jr. illustrated the importance of engaging policy issues to confront injustice, alluding to Jesus' parable of the Good Samaritan:

> On the one hand we are called to play the Good Samaritan on life's roadside, but that will be only an initial act. One day we must come to see that the whole Jericho Road must be transformed so that men and women will not be constantly beaten and robbed as they make their journey on life's highway. True compassion is more than flinging a coin to a beggar. It comes to see that an edifice which produces beggars needs restructuring.[6]

Of course we must compassionately bandage the wounds of those who have suffered injustice. But if, day after day, we encounter more people beaten alongside the road to Jericho, love of neighbor must compel us also to ask, "What's wrong with this road?" The victims of injustice along the road are most likely to have the answer. Once we know their solution, we should use whatever influence God has entrusted to us to change those conditions that are keeping people in cycles of brokenness, poverty, or marginalization.

When we hear a sermon about "stewardship," we tend to think

about money, and certainly we are responsible to God for the financial resources to which He has entrusted us and which ultimately belong to Him (Ps. 24:1). But being a good steward also compels us to leverage the influence God has given us to pursue *shalom*— which Tim Keller defines as "universal flourishing, wholeness, and delight"[7]—for our entire community, with an emphasis on those who are most vulnerable. Particularly in a democratic system of government, where elected officials tend to adjust their positions to win the support of the voters they need for reelection, we each have been entrusted with influence. That influence can be multiplied even beyond our own vote if we are willing to use our voice to winsomely persuade others.

For many Christians, there is an understandable concern about getting entangled in politics. While it is a mistake for the church to undermine its mission by becoming too closely identified with any political party's positions, we also believe God calls us to speak clearly about biblical principles that can form the basis of fair and effective government policy. We should do so, always, with civility and grace for those, both within and outside the church, who may disagree with us. We must consistently allow Scripture to guide us, not only in the policy ends that we pursue but also in the political means by which we pursue them.[8]

Fortunately, the Bible provides us with many models of advocating for justice before governmental authorities. Moses and Aaron pleaded with Pharaoh for their people's freedom. Queen Esther risked her life to intervene before King Xerxes began a genocide. Nehemiah, recognizing the unique access God had given him as the king's cupbearer, requested the opportunity to go to Jerusalem and rebuild the walls there. Prophets like Elijah, Jeremiah, Malachi, and, in the New Testament, John the Baptist called out the sins of rulers—both personal moral failings and systemic oppression of the poor and vulnerable. Even the apostle Paul made use of his Roman citizenship to insist upon just treatment (Acts 22:25).

As we seek to love our refugee neighbors—whether those in our own country or the majority of displaced people who are unlikely ever to reach our shores—we must carefully employ our rights as citizens as well.

THE CURRENT STATE OF REFUGEE POLICY

Following World War II, and the refugee crisis that it spurred, policies both in the United States and elsewhere moved toward greater compassion, as governments committed never again to return those seeking protection to a country where they would likely face persecution or death. In the decades that followed, the United States took in large numbers of refugees from Hungary, Vietnam, and Cuba on an *ad hoc* basis, then established the current refugee resettlement program with the passage of the Refugee Act of 1980. For decades the program has generally enjoyed broad bipartisan support.

Late in 2015, though, several factors converged, including unprecedented media focus as Syrians sought safety in unprecedented numbers in Europe, terrorist attacks in both France and California, and a US presidential campaign season that provided a strong incentive for media-hungry candidates to capitalize on voters' fears with brash rhetoric.

Quite suddenly, the question of refugee resettlement became a heated political controversy. On a single day in November, more than half of US governors announced their opposition to Syrian refugees being resettled into their states—though, because the Refugee Act places responsibility for refugee resettlement in the Executive Branch, the edicts ultimately had little practical effect, except, perhaps, for polarizing public opinion and instilling significant concern among already-resettled refugees who feared they would be deported back to a war zone.

Which Governors Oppose New Syrian Refugees?

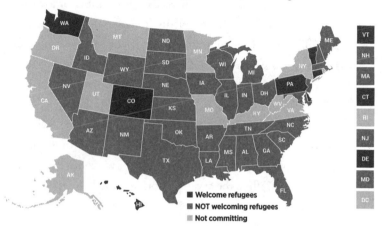

Source: Map published on CNN.com, Ashley Fantz and Ben Brumfield, "More than Half the Nation's Governors Say Syrian Refugees Not Welcome," CNN, November 16, 2015, http://www.cnn.com/ 2015/11/16/world/paris-attacks-syrian-refugees-backlash/.

Note: This map was posted on CNN.com on November 16, 2015.

A few days later, the House of Representatives hastily passed a broadly bipartisan bill to halt all refugee resettlement from both Syria and Iraq, a bill that our colleague Jenny Yang, World Relief's Vice President for Policy and Advocacy, warns would "abandon tens of thousands of carefully vetted, vulnerable refugees currently in the pipeline for resettlement, including many persecuted Christians." While, as of this writing, the bill seems unlikely to pass the US Senate—and faces the promise of a presidential veto if it were to pass— the state of the US refugee resettlement program is certainly tenuous, much more so than it has been at any time in recent history.

Similar debates are raging in other parts of the world. Europe, which received more than one million asylum seekers in 2015, has reestablished border checkpoints and barriers between countries that were removed decades ago. Political debates both within and between European countries have become heated as the continent considers how to respond to an unprecedented number of asylum seekers. In Canada, Prime Minister Justin Trudeau swept into power late in 2015 after promising to welcome *more* Syrian refugees. In the months after he was sworn in, he led an effort to resettle twenty-five thousand into Canada, where opposition was notably muted compared to in the United States.

Our conviction is that countries like the United States, which at its best moments has been a beacon of freedom for those fleeing persecution, should do more—not less—to welcome the most vulnerable refugees. While the seventy thousand total refugees from all parts of the world that the States admitted in 2015 may be a generous response in a normal time, this is not a normal time. We have urged this government to raise the number of refugees admitted to approximately the levels of 1980, when more than two hundred thousand refugees were welcomed.[9] We are prayerfully confident that American churches will step up to the challenge of welcoming as many as the government is willing to admit, driven by our biblical mandate to hospitality, the command to love our neighbors, and the opportunity to live out the Great Commission.

Even if this country were to welcome two hundred thousand refugees, it would still be only 1 percent of the world's refugees. We believe it is in our own national interest, as well as consistent with the character of a great and compassionate country, for our government to provide additional aid to the vast majority of refugees who will *not* be resettled, while leveraging our commitment to encourage allies in the Middle East and Europe to continue to receive those fleeing persecution.

As we pray that Christ followers will heed Jesus' commands to be peacemakers (Matt. 5:9), we also urge all governments to pursue peaceful resolutions to the conflicts in Syria and other countries that continue to expel refugees from their homes. How the government responds to each of these challenges, though—whether restricting in fear or expanding in magnanimity—will largely depend on elected officials whose decisions will be based on their assessments of their voting constituents' views.

We believe it is an urgent time for the church to speak up.

PRACTICAL WAYS TO ADVOCATE

Etymologically, *advocacy* is directly related to *voice*: to advocate is to "speak up for those who cannot speak for themselves" (Prov. 31:8). In reality, refugees *can* speak for themselves, and we ought to listen carefully to those most impacted by dysfunctional policies to find the solutions. As noncitizens, though, refugees are not yet able to vote, and thus may have a harder time getting the attention of elected officials focused on winning reelection. Those of us who are citizens can be stewards of that influence by speaking up for justice on behalf of and in coordination with those who have been displaced.

Public statements are one practical way to speak up for and with refugees. Late in 2015, as US public sentiment became more negative toward refugee resettlement, leaders from many prominent evangelical institutions—including the Southern Baptist Convention, the Assemblies of God, the Billy Graham Center for Evangelism at Wheaton College, the Willow Creek Association, World Relief, and World Vision, among others—released "A Christian Declaration on Caring for Refugees."[10] "Christians cannot remain silent," it asserts, affirming the dignity of each refugee as made in God's image, the call upon the church to love our refugee neighbors, and the importance of being driven by love, not fear. Hundreds of local pastors and Christian leaders affirmed the statement. Its organizers followed up with a summit that included talks from prominent evangelical leaders such as Rick Warren, Bill Hybels, Christine Caine, David Platt, and others. While not primarily focused on policy, the gathering certainly conveyed a clear message to legislators: evangelical Christians love and welcome refugees and do not want them to be scapegoated or the church's ability to minister to them curtailed.

Others have addressed elected officials directly. Senior leaders from the National Association of Evangelicals, the Southern Baptist Convention's Ethics and Religious Liberty Commission, the Council of Christian Colleges and Universities, the National Hispanic Christian Leadership Conference, and others joined together to form the Evangelical Immigration Table, a coalition focused on advocating for immigration policies consistent with biblical values. After the House of Representatives passed legislation in late 2015 to dramatically halt refugee resettlement from particular countries, the Evangelical Immigration Table sent a letter to each member of Congress, carefully articulating why they—and many of the millions of evangelical voters they represent in various evangelical denominations and parachurch ministries—believe that new restrictions on resettlement were inappropriate.[11]

Such advocacy is often even more effective at the local level. In Illinois, for example, pastors from more than a dozen churches, including some of the largest churches in the state, signed a letter to the state's two US senators, urging them *not* to vote to halt the refugee resettlement program, which had allowed many of their churches to welcome refugees locally in partnership with World Relief.[12]

In North Carolina, a few pastors met with their governor's staff after he announced his intention to prevent Syrian refugees from being resettled in the state. The pastors were able to explain how their churches had been involved in welcoming refugees, to help clear up some misconceptions, and to let the governor's staff know that they were genuinely praying for the governor as he considered this pressing issue. "I hoped the governor's staff would see there was a church of people ready to bear the responsibility of welcoming refugee families," says Matt Mig, community development and outreach pastor at The Summit Church, a Southern Baptist congregation with nine locations in and around Raleigh, Durham, and Chapel Hill. "The meeting was an opportunity not just for telling but for listening, and that helps me understand how to love and serve better."

Meeting with an elected official is more than just an effort to persuade them, it can also be ministry to them.[13] After all, in the United States at least, most elected officials profess to be Christ followers, and many are sincerely committed to applying biblical truth to the complex legislative decisions that they face. Like many other Americans, some may just genuinely never have considered that the Bible speaks so clearly to the plight of refugees and other immigrants. The Evangelical Immigration Table has developed a Bible-reading guide—the "I Was a Stranger" Challenge—which lists forty Bible passages related to God's heart for foreigners. In addition to distributing hundreds of thousands of these bookmarks as a discipleship tool within local churches, some pastors also dropped them off at their legislators' offices, inviting elected officials to take up the call.

Beyond directly reaching out to elected officials, we can advocate through media as well. For example, Dr. Russell Moore, president of the Southern Baptist Convention's Ethics and Religious Liberty Commission, penned an op-ed column for the *Washington Post*, explaining his beliefs that compassion for Syrian refugees and security are not mutually exclusive. "We cannot forget our brothers and sisters in peril. And we cannot seal ourselves off from our mission field," he wrote.[14]

Similarly, local pastors Bob Roberts of Northwood Church, in Keller, Texas, and David Daniels of Pantego Bible Church, in Fort Worth, reminded readers of the *Fort Worth Star-Telegram* of Jesus' words, encouraging a response rooted in hospitality and love for displaced people.[15] Bryant Wright, senior pastor of Johnson Ferry Baptist Church in suburban Atlanta, spoke with Fox News about the biblical principles that led his church, in partnership with World Relief Atlanta, to welcome and walk alongside a Syrian refugee family, even after the state's governor had issued an executive order to block state agencies from providing any assistance to Syrian refugees.[16]

While most of us will likely not have the opportunity to appear on a national news program, anyone can submit a letter to the editor of their local newspaper, which elected officials are quite likely to see and to take as an indication of the opinions of their constituents. We can also send emails or letters to our congressmen and women, or call their offices and leave a message expressing our views. Believe it or not, hearing from voters really *does* influence how legislators vote, as they often use communication from constituents to take the pulse of the people they are trying to represent. In the days after the House of Representatives voted to restrict refugee resettlement in November 2015, Christians, mobilized by WeWelcomeRefugees.com, sent more than ten thousand messages to their elected officials, which may be one reason the Senate failed to move the legislation forward.

Other churches found creative ways to advocate: Christ's Church of the Valley in Royersford, Pennsylvania, focused a Sunday service on God's heart for refugees, then took to social media to advocate, asking attendees to post a hash-tagged selfie with a "We Welcome

Refugees" sign to Twitter, Facebook, or Instagram. Church-based volunteers with World Relief's office in Wheaton, Illinois, took a more old-school approach to expressing their support for refugees and posted yard signs that declare, "We Are Not Afraid" and "We Welcome Refugees."

If the church is to take up the invitation—and the opportunity—to love our refugee neighbors, advocacy is an integral component, because policies directly impact the well-being of these neighbors. So long as governmental authorities allow refugees to continue to be allowed in, though, local churches can and, we argue, ought to reflect the love of Christ to these newcomers to our communities in tangible ways as well. As the church demonstrates love for refugees, both through advocacy and in practical acts of service, we also testify to the character of our God.

CHAPTER 11

"A SHINING CITY ON A HILL"

In his farewell address to the nation in 1989, President Ronald Reagan, borrowing a line from Jesus, described the United States as a "shining city on a hill" for those seeking freedom, a place "teeming with people of all kinds living in harmony and peace" whose "doors were open to anyone with the will and the heart to get here."[1]

Over the course of centuries, the United States certainly has been a place of refuge for many fleeing persecution and "yearning to breathe free," which is an honorable legacy.[2] But when Jesus talked about a "city on a hill," He was not referring to the United States of America, nor to any other nation-state. Jesus told His followers that *they*—those early disciples who would go on to form the earliest church—were the light of the world, which, like a city atop a hill, could not be hidden (Matt. 5:14). "Let your light shine before others," Jesus told them, "that they may see your good deeds and glorify your Father in heaven" (Matt. 5:16).

Faced with a global refugee crisis unprecedented in recorded history, now is the moment for the church to shine, not to hide our light. Millions of displaced people, desperate for hope yet reviled and feared by many, will decide what they think of Jesus based on how His followers throughout the world respond to this crisis, whether with welcome, love, and advocacy, or with apathy, fear, and scapegoating.

Across the nation and the world, local churches are seeing this moment of crisis as a chance to live out Jesus' instructions, shining their light, so others may look to and glorify God.

Many of these ministries are led by relatively small churches whose pastors and leaders are themselves refugees or other immigrants. Pastor Raed Awabdeh, for example—whose grandfather discovered Jesus through a Christian and Missionary Alliance missionary in southern Syria—now pastors the Christian and Missionary Alliance–affiliated Arabic Church of Sacramento, California, which serves about twelve hundred refugees per year through its Arab-American Center, the vast majority of whom are Iraqi refugees. At least seventy-five of them have decided to follow Jesus. Pastor Durmomo Gary was persecuted in Sudan, where he worked as a Bible translator, escaped to Egypt, and then was resettled as a refugee in the United States, where he has served the Sudanese Community Church in Wheaton, Illinois, while also pursuing his master's degree at the Moody Bible Institute. Dr. Stoney Cem, born in Burma, serves as a caseworker for World Relief Jacksonville while also pastoring the Canaan Chin Baptist Church in Jacksonville, Florida.

While their vibrant ministry is not always well known to majority culture Christians even within the same cities, these integral members of the body of Christ are indeed shining examples of welcoming strangers in Jesus' name. Many others—of every ethnicity, language, and denomination throughout the world, pastors *and laypeople* from every walk of life—are similarly investing their lives on behalf of the displaced and the vulnerable.

The reality, though, is that the church as a whole has a mixed record in how we respond to refugees. As many national Christian leaders in the United States call for compassion and as denominations see remarkable fruit as a result of ministry to refugees, others have been outspoken in calling on governments to restrict their entry.

At the local church level, the statistics are discouraging: while, as of September 2015, most Americans supported a US government plan to increase the overall number of refugees resettled here, white evangelical Christians were opposed to the plan by a two-to-one margin.[3] While 86 percent of American Protestant pastors surveyed by Life-Way Research in 2016 affirmed that "Christians have a responsibility to care sacrificially for refugees and foreigners," less than one in ten said their church was currently involved in caring locally for refugees, and less than one in five was serving refugees overseas.[4] Nearly half acknowledged that, among the members of their congregation, there was a sense of fear about refugees coming to the United States.[5]

Too often, the church has allowed politicians or media who describe refugees as a menace to speak for us on these questions. If we cheer them on, or if we merely stay silent, millions of vulnerable, displaced people throughout the world will associate Christians— and the Jesus we claim to follow—with apathy or, worse, hostility toward refugees.

"You are the salt of the earth," Jesus told His followers, each of us—you. He continued:

> *But if the salt loses its saltiness, how can it be made salty again?*
> *It is no longer good for anything, except to be thrown out and*
> *trampled underfoot.*
>
> *You are the light of the world. A town built on a hill cannot*
> *be hidden. Neither do people light a lamp and put it under*
> *a bowl. Instead they put it on its stand, and it gives light to*

*everyone in the house. In the same way, let your light shine
before others, that they may see your good deeds and glorify your
Father in heaven.* (Matt. 5:13–16)

Our ultimate hope for this book is that the church would shine
its light through the refugee crisis. As we access the same power that
rose Jesus from the dead, we pray God's people would rise up as
never before to welcome strangers, each doing what God has called
all of us to do:

To bind up the brokenhearted.

To love our neighbors.

To do justice.

To love mercy.

To pray without ceasing.

To practice hospitality, and to learn to receive the hospitality of
others.

Maybe just to take a plate of cookies across the street, trusting that
a smile can overcome a language barrier.

To write a letter to a congressperson, or gently speak up at the work-
place water cooler when someone repeats a false rumor about refugees.

Perhaps to forego a vacation to give sacrificially for those whose
travels were involuntary.

To stand with our persecuted brothers and sisters, mourning with
those who mourn, rejoicing with those who rejoice.

To proclaim the love of Christ in word and deed to those who do
not yet know Him.

Our prayer is ultimately that, as the church lets her light shine
and steps into the good works God has "prepared in advance for us
to do" (Eph. 2:10), the displaced of our world will praise our Father
in heaven.

Soli Deo Gloria.

U.S. REFUGEE RESETTLEMENT PROGRAM CONTACTS

If this book inspires you to take one step, we hope it will be to connect to a refugee in your community. Our local offices throughout the United States are eager to partner with both individuals and local churches to welcome refugees and other immigrants. Where there is not a World Relief office, one of the other national resettlement agencies may have an affiliate.

WORLD RELIEF-AFFILIATED US OFFICES

For the most up-to-date listing of local offices and contact information, please visit www.worldrelief.org.

CALIFORNIA

World Relief Garden Grove: www.worldreliefgardengrove.org,
714-210-4730
World Relief Modesto: www.worldreliefmodesto.org,
209-491-2712
World Relief Sacramento: www.worldreliefsacramento.org,
916-978-2650

FLORIDA

World Relief Jacksonville: www.worldreliefjacksonville.org,
  904-448-0733
World Relief Miami: www.worldrelief.org/miami, 305-541-8320
World Relief Tampa: www.worldrelieftampa.org, 727-859-1650

GEORGIA

World Relief Atlanta (Stone Mountain): www.worldreliefatlanta.
  org, 404-294-4352

IDAHO

World Relief Boise: www.worldreliefboise.org, 208-323-4964

ILLINOIS

World Relief Aurora: www.worldreliefaurora.org, 630-906-9546
World Relief Chicago: www.worldreliefchicago.org, 773-583-9191
World Relief DuPage (Wheaton): www.worldreliefdupage.org,
  630-462-7566
World Relief Moline: www.worldreliefmoline.org, 309-764-2279

MARYLAND

World Relief Anne Arundel: www.worldreliefannearundel.org,
  410-760-4514
World Relief Baltimore Immigration Legal Clinic: www.worldre-
  lief.org/baltimore, 410-244-0002

MINNESOTA

Arrive Ministries (Richfield): www.arriveministries.org,
  612-798-4332

NORTH CAROLINA

World Relief Durham: www.worldreliefdurham.org,
  919-286-3496

World Relief High Point: www.worldreliefhighpoint.org,
  336-887-9007

OHIO

World Relief Akron: www.worldreliefakron.org, 234-334-5190
World Relief Columbus: www.worldreliefcolumbus.org,
  614-337-2448

SOUTH CAROLINA

World Relief Spartanburg: www.worldreliefspartanburg.org,
  864-642-2626

TENNESSEE

World Relief Memphis: www.worldreliefmemphis.org,
  901-341-0220
World Relief Nashville: www.worldreliefnashville.org,
  615-833-7735

TEXAS

World Relief Fort Worth: www.worldrelieffortworth.org,
  817-924-0748

WASHINGTON

World Relief Seattle (Kent): www.worldreliefseattle.org,
  253-277-1121
World Relief Spokane: www.worldreliefspokane.org,
  509-484-9829
World Relief Tri-Cities (Richland): www.worldrelieftricities.org,
  509-734-5477

WISCONSIN

World Relief Fox Valley (Oshkosh): www.worldrelieffoxvalley.org,
  920-231-3600

If World Relief is not yet located in your community, it is possible that we could consider opening a new site. When exploring potential new sites, we look first and foremost for places where local churches want to be empowered to welcome refugees. We also consult with local, state, and federal governmental entities to ensure that we set refugees up for success by resettling them into locations with job opportunities, relatively affordable housing and costs of living, and a welcoming community. If you would like more information on potential new World Relief locations, please contact NewSites@wr.org.

OTHER RESETTLEMENT AGENCIES

Church World Service: www.cwsglobal.org, 800-297-1516

Episcopal Migration Ministries: www.episcopalmigration ministries.org, 212-716-6000

Ethiopian Community Development Council: www.ecdcus.org, 703-685-0510

Hebrew Immigrant Aid Society (HIAS): www.hias.org, 301-844-7300

International Rescue Committee: www.rescue.org, 212-551-3000

Lutheran Immigration and Refugee Service: www.lirs.org, 410-230-2700

US Conference of Catholic Bishops: www.usccb.org/mrs, 202-541-3352

US Committee for Refugees and Immigrants: www.refugees.org, 703-310-1130

For a full map of all US resettlement agencies, including local contact information, please visit http://bit.ly/RefugeeResettlementMap.

NOTES

Chapter 1: An Unprecedented Global Crisis

1. "UNHCR Global Trends: Forced Displacement in 2014," United Nations High Commissioner for Refugees, http://unhcr.org/556725e69.html#_ga=1.2 3600890.1718187515.1441033927.

2. Ibid.

3. Karen Miller Pensiero, "Aylan Kurdi and the Photos That Change History," *Wall Street Journal*, September 11, 2015, http://www.wsj.com/articles/ aylan-kurdi-and-the-photos-that-change-history-1442002594.

4. Bill Hybels, *Courageous Leadership* (Grand Rapids: Zondervan, 2002), 27.

5. Michael Gerson, "The Children among Syria's Ruins," *Washington Post*, October 15, 2015, https://www.washingtonpost.com/opinions/syrian-children- among-the-ruins/2015/10/15/8d0510de-7360-11e5-8d93-0af317ed58c9_ story.html.

6. Pamela Duncan, "More than 1 Million People Have Sought EU Asylum So Far in 2015," *The Guardian*, December 9, 2015, http://www.theguardian.com /world/2015/dec/09/more-than-1-million-people-have-sought-eu-asylum-so- far-in-2015.

7. UNHCR Global Trends, 21.

8. While we absolutely believe that the Bible ought to inform how we respond to larger issues of immigration, including illegal immigration, our primary emphasis with this book is specifically focused on refugees, and we will note intersections with other immigration issues only tangentially. For a review of broader immigration issues, we recommend Matthew's book, coauthored with Jenny Hwang Yang, *Welcoming the Stranger: Justice, Compassion & Truth in the Immigration Debate* (Downers Grove, IL: InterVarsity, 2009).

9. "Bloomberg Politics National Poll," Selzer & Company, November 18, 2015, http://www.scribd.com/doc/290213526/Bloomberg-Politics-National-Poll-v3 -Nov-18-2015.

Chapter 2: Jesus Was a Refugee: Thinking Biblically about Migration

1. "Evangelical Views on Immigration," LifeWay Research, February 2015, http://www.lifewayresearch.com/files/2015/03/Evangelical-Views-on-Immigration-Report.pdf.

2. Ibid.

3. Matthew Soerens and Jenny Hwang Yang, *Welcoming the Stranger: Justice, Compassion & Truth in the Immigration Debate* (Downers Grove, IL: InterVarsity, 2009), 83.

4. Walter C. Kaiser Jr., "Leviticus," *The New Interpreter's Bible: Genesis to Leviticus,* vol. 1 (Nashville: Abingdon, 1994), 1135.

5. Orlando O. Espín, "Immigration and Theology: Reflections by an Implicated Theologian," *Perspectivas: Occasional Papers* (Hispanic Theological Initiative), no. 10 (Fall 2006): 46–47.

6. LifeWay Research, "Evangelical Views on Immigration."

7. "Church Sign: Christmas: A Story about a Middle East Family Seeking Refuge," KMPS-TV Fox 9, December 8, 2015, http://www.fox9.com/news/56360761-story.

8. Christine D. Pohl and Ben Donley, "Responding to Refugees: Christian Reflections on a Global Crisis," *Crossroads Monograph Series on Faith and Public Policy* (Wynnewood, PA: Evangelicals for Social Action, 2000), 2.

9. Fleur S. Houston, *You Shall Love the Stranger as Yourself: The Bible, Refugees, and Asylum* (New York: Routledge, 2015), 136.

10. M. Daniel Carroll Rodas, *Christians at the Border: Immigration, the Church, and the Bible* (Grand Rapids: Baker Academic, 2008), 118.

11. There certainly were both risk and cost involved for the Samaritan, much more so than for those who would seek to serve resettled refugees in North America today.

12. Carroll Rodas, *Christians at the Border*, 65–71.

13. Russell Moore, *Onward: Engaging the Culture without Losing the Gospel* (Nashville: B&H, 2015), 120.

14. Ibid., 115.

15. For more thorough analyses of the population control roots and philosophies of several of the most outspoken groups advocating for tighter restrictions on refugee resettlement and immigration generally, see Mario H. Lopez, "Hijacking Immigration," *Human Life Review,* fall 2012, http://www.human-

lifereview.com/hijacking-immigration/ and J. C. Derrick, "Friend or Foe?," *WORLD Magazine,* March 9, 2013, http://www.worldmag.com/2013/02/ friend_or_foe.

16. For example, economist Alex Nowrasteh has carefully detailed the economic flaws in analyses by the Federation for American Immigration Reform and the Center for Immigration Studies. See, respectively, Alex Nowrasteh, "A Fair Criticism," Competitive Enterprise Institute, October 25, 2011, http:// cei.org/sites/default/files/Alex%20Nowrasteh%20-%20WebMemo%20 -%20A%20FAIR%20Criticism.pdf and Alex Nowrasteh, "Center for Immigration Studies Report Exaggerates Immigrant Welfare Use," *Cato at Liberty,* Cato Institute, September 2, 2015, http://www.cato.org/blog/ center-immigration-studies-exaggerates-immigrant-welfare-use.

17. Michael Gerson, "How the Dream Act Transcends Politics," *Washington Post,* December 7, 2010, http://www.washingtonpost.com/wp-dyn/content/ article/2010/12/06/AR2010120605406.html.

18. William Cadigan, "Christian Persecution Reached Record High in 2015," CNN, January 17, 2016, http://www.cnn.com/2016/01/17/world/christian-persecution-2015/index.html.

19. Sarah Eekhoff Zylstra, "It's Official: Terrorists Are Now the Persecuted Church's Greatest Threat," *Christianity Today,* October 2015, http://www. christianitytoday.com/gleanings/2015/october/international-religious-free-dom-report-2014-state-dept.html.

20. "2014 International Religious Freedom Report: Executive Summary," US Department of State, 2015, http://www.state.gov/documents/organiza-tion/238390.pdf, 1.

21. John Kerry, "Remarks on Daesh and Genocide," US Department of State, March 17, 2016, http://www.state.gov/secretary/remarks/2016/03/254782 .htm.

22. Sandy Barron et al., *Refugees from Burma: Their Backgrounds and Refugee Expe-riences* (Washington, DC: Center for Applied Linguistics, Cultural Orienta-tion Resource Center, 2007).

23. "World Watch List 2015: Nigeria #10," *Open Doors,* 2015, https://www. opendoorsusa.org/file_viewer.php?id=1458.

24. Morgan Lee, "Here's Where America's 338,000 Christian Refugees Come From," *Christianity Today,* November 2015, http://www.christianitytoday. com/gleanings/2015/november/heres-where-americas-338000-christian-refugees-have-come.html.

25. Refugee Processing Center of the US Department of State's Bureau of Population, Refugees, and Migration, http://www.wrapsnet.org/Reports/Interactive Reporting/tabid/393/EnumType/Report/Default.aspx?ItemPath=/rpt_Web ArrivalsReports/MX%20-%20Arrivals%20by%20Nationality%20and%20 Religion.

26. Ibid.

27. "Immigrants: A Position Paper of Ethnic America Network," *Ethnic America Network*, 2014, http://ethnicamerica.com/wpv1/wp-content/up-loads/2014/09/EAN-immigrants-paper-September-17-2014.pdf, 3.

28. Enoch Wan, *Diaspora Missiology: Theory, Methodology, and Practice* (Portland, OR: Institute of Diaspora Studies, 2011), 5.

29. J. D. Payne, *Strangers Next Door: Immigration, Migration and Mission* (Downers Grove, IL: InterVarsity, 2012), 63.

30. Pew Research Center, *Global Religious Landscape*, December 18, 2012, http://www.pewforum.org/files/2014/01/global-religion-full.pdf, 49.

31. Gary Barnes, "Why Don't They Listen?," *Christianity Today*, September 2003, http://www.christianitytoday.com/ct/2003/september/2.50.html?share=73kz7 5mDJQ6OvDxmZHgBLk5NBA12vXkZ.

32. "Manila Manifesto," Lausanne Movement, 1989, https://www.lausanne.org/content/manifesto/the-manila-manifesto.

33. Abby Stocker, "The Craziest Statistic You'll Read about North American Missions," *Christianity Today*, August 19, 2013, http://www.christianitytoday.com/ct/2013/august-web-only/non-christians-who-dont-know-christians.html.

34. Cited in Manya Brachear Pashman, "Wheaton College Could Face Long-Term Fallout over Professor Controversy," *Chicago Tribune*, February 22, 2016, http://www.chicagotribune.com/news/ct-wheaton-college-professor-fallout-met-20160222-story.html. Notably, African-American Protestants surveyed are significantly more likely to know people of other religious traditions. We have been unable to verify data for Christians of other ethnicities.

35. J. D. Payne, "Pressure Point #5: International Migration," *Missiologically Thinking*, June 6, 2013, http://www.jdpayne.org/2013/06/06/pressure-point-5-international-migration/.

36. Juan Martinez, "Latin American Theology," Wheaton College Theology Conference: Global Theology in Evangelical Perspective, April 7, 2011, http://espace.wheaton.edu/media/wetn/BITH/mp3/110407Martinez.mp3.

37. We have borrowed and adapted this idea from Moore, *Onward: Engaging the Culture without Losing the Gospel*, 206.

38. Ibid., 207.

39. Albert Mohler, "The Briefing," October 22, 2014, http://www.albertmohler.com/?p=33009.

40. Michael Lipka, "A Closer Look at America's Rapidly Growing Religious 'Nones,'" Pew Research Center, May 13, 2015, http://www.pewresearch.org/fact-tank/2015/05/13/a-closer-look-at-americas-rapidly-growing-religious-nones/.

41. Wesley Granberg-Michaelson, "The Hidden Immigration Impact on American Churches," *Washington Post*, September 23, 2013, https://www.washingtonpost.com/national/on-faith/commentary-the-hidden-immigration-impact-on-american-churches/2013/09/23/0bd53b74-2484-11e3-9372-92606241ae9c_story.html.

42. Joseph Castleberry, *The New Pilgrims: How Immigrants Are Renewing America's Faith and Values* (Franklin, TN: Worthy, 2015), 99.

43. Timothy Tennent, "Christian Perspective on Immigration," Seedbed, June 22, 2011, https://www.youtube.com/watch?v=WHx95cuXpUE&noredirect=1.

44. "Pastor Views on Refugees," LifeWay Research, January 2016, http://lifewayresearch.com/wp-content/uploads/2016/02/Pastor-Views-on-Refugees-Final-Report-January-2016.pdf.

45. "New LifeWay Research Finds Widespread Support for Immigration Reform among Pastors," LifeWay Research, November 18, 2014, http://blog.lifeway.com/newsroom/2014/11/18/new-lifeway-research-finds-widespread-support-for-immigration-reform-among-pastors/.

Chapter 3: The Human Face of Forced Migration: The Power of a Story

1. Mary Pipher, *The Middle of Everywhere: The World's Refugees Come to Our Town* (New York: Harcourt, 2002), 331.

2. Chamamanda Ngozi Adichie, "The Danger of a Single Story," TED Talk, October 2009, https://www.ted.com/talks/chimamanda_adichie_the_danger_of_a_single_story/transcript?language=en.

3. Islam is divided between two major traditions, Shiite and Sunni, analogous in some ways to the division between Catholic and Protestant Christians. Sunnis and Shiites share many core theological beliefs, but diverge on some important doctrines. In particular, Sunnis see the Koran and the teachings of the Prophet

Mohamad as their authority, while Shiites also revere the teachings of subsequent leaders related to Mohamad, such as his son-in-law, Ali. While most Muslims globally are Sunni, Shiites form the majority in Iran, Iraq, and a few other countries, each of which also has a significant Sunni minority.

In Syria, Sunni Muslims form the majority of the population. Most Sunnis are Arabic speakers and ethnically Arab, but about 15 percent of Sunnis are Kurds, an ethnic minority scattered throughout several countries in the region, without a state of its own. The Assad regime are Alawites, a Shiite-related group that, at least prior to the civil war, formed slightly more than one-tenth of the Syrian population.

An additional one-tenth of the Syrian population, approximately, are from historic Christian groups, primarily in the Orthodox and Catholic traditions. Syrian Christians and other religious minorities, such as the Druze, have generally been protected by the Assad government.

4. Karen Yourish, K. K. Rebecca Lai, and Derek Watkins, "Death in Syria," *New York Times*, September 14, 2015, http://www.nytimes.com/interactive/2015/09/14/world/middleeast/syria-war-deaths.html; Chris York and George Bowden, "Syria Civil War Death Toll Paints a Horrifyingly Complex Picture," *Huffington Post UK*, October 31, 2015, http://www.huffingtonpost. co.uk/2015/10/31/syrian-civil-war-death-_n_8440378.html.

5. Hugh Naylor, "Islamic State Has Killed Many Syrians, but Assad's Forces Have Killed More," *Washington Post*, September 5, 2015, https://www. washingtonpost.com/world/islamic-state-has-killed-many-syrians-but-assads-forces-have-killed-even-more/2015/09/05/b8150d0c-4d85-11e5-80c2-106ea7fb80d4_story.html.

6. Hataipreuk Rkasnuam and Jeanne Batalova, "Vietnamese Immigrants in the United States," *Migration Policy Institute*, August 25, 2014, http://www. migrationpolicy.org/article/vietnamese-immigrants-united-states.

7. Hajer Naili, "100,000 Bhutanese Refugees Resettled: First Family Recall Their Journey to the USA," *International Organization for Migration*, November 19, 2015, http://weblog.iom.int/100000-bhutanese-refugees-resettled-first-family -recall-their-journey-usa.

8. We'll describe a number of practical opportunities for churches and volunteers to interact relationally with refugees in chapter 7.

Chapter 4: No Fear in Love: Grappling with Genuine Concerns over Refugee Resettlement

1. "Election 2016 Preview 2016," Barna Group, May 2015, https://www.barna. org/barna-update/culture/719-election-2016-preview-the-faith-factor, 4. See

also "Wide Partisan Differences over the Issues That Matter in 2014," Pew Research Center, September 12, 2014, http://www.people-press.org/2014/09/12/wide-partisan-differences-over-the-issues-that-matter-in-2014.

2. Tim Annett, "Illegal Immigrants and the Economy," *Wall Street Journal*, April 13, 2006, http://www.wsj.com/articles/SB114477669441223067.

3. "Is Migration Good for the Economy?" Organization for Economic Cooperation and Development, May 2014, http://www.oecd.org/migration/OECD%20Migration%20Policy%20Debates%20Numero%202.pdf, 1.

4. James Pethokoukis, "Dynamic Immigration Scoring: Score One for Cato and Marco Rubio," *AEIdeas*, April 9, 2013, https://www.aei.org/publication/dynamic-immigration-scoring-score-one-for-cato-and-marco-rubio/.

5. Lisa Beilfuss, "Some of Syria's Neighbors See an Economic Boost from Refugees," *Wall Street Journal*, December 31, 2015, http://blogs.wsj.com/economics/2015/12/31/some-of-syrias-neighbors-see-an-economic-boost-from-refugees/,

6. Elizabeth Matsangou, "Refugees Are an Economic Benefit, Not Burden, to Europe," *World Finance*, November 2, 2015, http://www.worldfinance.com/infrastructure-investment/government-policy/refugees-are-an-economic-benefit-not-burden-to-europe.

7. Kalena Cortes, "Are Refugees Different from Economic Immigrants? Some Empirical Evidence of the Heterogeneity of Immigrant Groups in the United States," *Institute for the Study of Labor*, March 2004, http://papers.ssrn.com/sol3/papers.cfm?abstract_id=524605.

8. Randy Capps, Kathleen Newland, Susan Fratzke, Susanna Groves, Michael Fix, Margie McHugh, and Gregory Auclair, *The Integration Outcomes of U.S. Refugees: Successes and Challenges* (Washington, DC: Migration Policy Institute, 2015), 16.

9. Paul Hagstrom, "The Fiscal Impact of Refugee Resettlement in the Mohawk Valley," Hamilton College, June 2000, http://www.hamilton.edu/Levitt/pdfs/hagstrom_refugee.pdf.

10. John Cassidy, "The Economics of Syrian Refugees," *The New Yorker*, November 18, 2015, http://www.newyorker.com/news/john-cassidy/the-economics-of-syrian-refugees.

11. Maya Federman, David Harrington, and Kathy Krynski, "Vietnamese Manicurists: Are Immigrants Displacing Natives or Finding New Nails to Polish?" *Industrial and Labor Relations Review* 59 (January 2006): 315.

12. "Impact of Refugees in Central Ohio: 2015 Report," Community Research Partners, January 2016, http://www.communityresearchpartners.org/wp-content/uploads/2016/01/IMPACT-OF-REFUGEES-ON-CENTRAL-OHIO_2015SP.pdf, 17.

13. Ibid.

14. Brian Solomon, "Google Just Passed Apple as the World's Most Valuable Company," *Forbes*, February 1, 2016, http://www.forbes.com/sites/brian-solomon/2016/02/01/google-just-passed-apple-as-the-worlds-most-valuable-company/#4f7e06ab16f9.

15. Stephanie Strom, "Billionaire Aids Charity That Aided Him," *New York Times*, October 24, 2009, http://www.nytimes.com/2009/10/25/us/25donate.html?scp=1&sq=brin&st=cse&_r=0.

16. James Hoffmeier, *The Immigration Crisis: Immigrants, Aliens, and the Bible* (Wheaton, IL: Crossway, 2009), 96.

17. These statistics from 2006 through 2015 and all other demographic information in this section are from the online database of the US State Department's Refugee Processing Center, www.wrapsnet.org.

18. Those who are "Christian," as classified by the US government, are based on self-identification and include those from a broad range of Christian traditions, including Roman Catholic, Orthodox, and those of various Protestant denominations, as well as some non-Trinitarian religious traditions that consider themselves Christians, such as Jehovah's Witnesses and Mormons.

19. It should also be noted that the number of Christian refugees arriving from Syria, in particular, who had been admitted as of early 2016 was quite low, only a few percent of the total. One significant reason for this is because the screening process for refugees being considered for resettlement to the United States is very thorough and lengthy, and the relatively few Syrian refugees who had been admitted as of early 2016—about 2,700—were generally individuals who fled the country early in the civil war that began in 2011, fleeing from the government of Bashar al-Assad. While Mr. al-Assad's indiscriminate bombings have certainly killed and displaced Christians, they have not been uniquely targeted; in fact, many Syrian Christians experienced a certain degree of protection under the Assad regime. Daesh, also known as the "Islamic State," ISIS, or ISIL, arose only in 2013, and has, sadly, particularly persecuted Christians, but most Christians who have fled the country to escape Daesh have not yet completed the lengthy US refugee resettlement screening process.

Additionally, many of those Christians who have fled the country went to Lebanon—rather than Turkey, Jordan, or Egypt—but the US government has been unable for many months to process refugees out of Lebanon because of security concerns.

Furthermore, because Syrians of Christian origin tended to be better off economically than the average Syrian Muslim, they also would be more likely to have tourist visas to allow them to fly to the United States, Europe, or elsewhere, where they could request asylum without making a dangerous journey via land to a neighboring country where conditions are very stark.

20. "Muslim Americans: No Signs of Growth in Alienation or Support for Extremism," Pew Research Center, August 30, 2011, http://www.people-press. org/files/legacy-pdf/Muslim%20American%20Report%2010-02-12%20fix. pdf, 4.

21. John Azumah, "Challenging Radical Islam: An Explanation of Islam's Relation to Terrorism and Violence," *First Things*, January 2015, http://www.first things.com/article/2015/01/challenging-radical-islam.

22. Ed Stetzer, "3 Reasons Christians Should Back Religious Freedom for All," *Religion News Service*, December 30, 2015, http://www.religionnews. com/2015/12/30/3-reasons-christians-back-religious-freedom-commentary/.

23. Afshin Ziafat, "The Cost of Following Christ: One Man's Journey from Islam to Christianity," Ethics and Religious Liberty Commission, April 2, 2015, https://www.youtube.com/watch?v=xFO6GRMa7mc&feature=youtu.be.

24. Robert Farley, "9/11 Hijackers and Student Visas," May 10, 2013, FactCheck. org, http://www.factcheck.org/2013/05/911-hijackers-and-student-visas.

25. Abigail Abrams, "Paris Attacks 2015: Named Terrorists All European Nationals, Not Syrian Refugees," *International Business Times*, November 19, 2015, http://www.ibtimes.com/paris-attack-2015-named-terrorists-all-european- nationals-not-syrian-refugees-2191677; Alissa J. Rubin and Rick Gladstone, "Brussels Attack Lapse Acknowledged by Belgian Officials," *New York Times*, March 24, 2016, http://www.nytimes.com/2016/03/25/world/europe/ brussels-attacks.html; please note that, as this book went to press, some details of the identities of the perpetrators in these attacks were still unconfirmed.

26. Jack Healy, "Visa Form Adds Details on How San Bernardino Attacker Met Wife," *New York Times*, December 22, 2015, http://www.nytimes. com/2015/12/23/us/san-bernardino-attacker-described-on-visa-forms-how- he-met-wife.html.

27. National Association of Evangelicals, "NAE Calls for Continued Resettlement of Refugees," November 17, 2015, http://nae.net/nae-calls-for-continued- resettlement-of-refugees/.

28. Evan Perez, "FBI Director James Comey Balks at Refugee Legislation," CNN, November 19, 2015, http://www.cnn.com/2015/11/19/politics/fbi-director-james-comey-refugee-legislation/index.html.

29. Jeremy Diamond, "Entering the U.S. as Refugees Would Be the Hardest Way for Would-Be Terrorists," CNN, November 20, 2015, http://www.cnn.com/2015/11/20/politics/paris-attack-refugee-visa-waiver/.

30. Mark Johanson, "US Received Record Number of Visitors in 2012 Thanks to These 15 Countries," *International Business Times*, June 11, 2013, http://www.ibtimes.com/us-received-record-number-visitors-2012-thanks-these-15-countries-1300347.

31. Alex Nowrasteh, "Syrian Refugees Don't Pose a Serious Security Threat," *Cato at Liberty*, November 18, 2015, http://www.cato.org/blog/syrian-refugees-dont-pose-serious-security-threat.

32. Ibid.

33. "Homegrown Extremism 2001–2015," New America, August 2015, http://securitydata.newamerica.net/extremists/analysis.html.

34. Ibid.

35. David Bier, "The Boston Bombers Were Not Refugees—Neither Was the Paris Attacker," Niskanen Center, November 17, 2015, https://niskanencenter.org/blog/the-boston-bombers-were-not-refugees-neither-was-the-paris-attacker/.

36. Jessica Zuckerman, Steven Bucci, and Jame Jay Carafano, "60 Terrorist Plots since 9/11: Continued Lessons in Domestic Counterterrorism," The Heritage Foundation, July 22, 2013, http://www.heritage.org/research/reports/2013/07/60-terrorist-plots-since-911 continued-lessons-in-domestic-counterterrorism.

37. Morgan Lee, "Morocco Declaration: Muslim Nations Should Protect Christians from Persecution," *Christianity Today*, January 27, 2016, http://www.christianitytoday.com/gleanings/2016/january/marrakesh-declaration-muslim-nations-christian-persecution.html.

38. Jacquelien van Stekelenburg and Bert Klandermans, "Radicalization," *Identity and Participation in Culturally Diverse Societies*, ed. A. E. Azzi, X. Chryssochoou, B. Klandermans, and B. Simon. (Oxford: Wiley-Blackwell, 2010), 184. See also Kamaldeep Bhui, Sokratis Dinos, and Edgar Jones, "Psychological Process and Pathways to Radicalization," *Journal of Bioterrorism and Biodefense*, 2012, http://www.omicsonline.org/psychological-process-and-pathways-to-radicalization-2157-2526.S5-003.pdf.

39. Rich Stearns, GC2 Summit Leadership Meeting, Billy Graham Center for Evangelism at Wheaton College, December 17, 2015.

40. "Crime Statistics," Federal Bureau of Investigation, https://www.fbi.gov/stats-services/crimestats; "Homegrown Extremism 2001–2015," New America.

41. C. S. Lewis, *The Lion, the Witch, and the Wardrobe* (New York: HarperCollins, 1978), 80.

Chapter 5: From Strangers to Neighbors to Family: Understanding Refugee Resettlement

1. Jamie Dean, "Who Is My Neighbor?," *WORLD Magazine*, November 14, 2014, http://www.worldmag.com/2015/10/who_is_my_neighbor/.

2. Richard Fausset, "Refugee Crisis in Syria Raises Fears in South Carolina," *New York Times*, September 25, 2015, http://www.nytimes.com/2015/09/26/us/refugee-crisis-in-syria-raises-fears-in south-carolina.html.

3. Refugee Processing Center of the US Department of State's Bureau of Population, Refugees, and Migration, http://www.wrapsnet.org.

4. United Nations High Commissioner for Refugees, *UNHCR Resettlement Handbook*, 2011, http://www.unhcr.org/cgi-bin/texis/vtx/home/opendocPD-FViewer.html?docid=46f7c0ee2&query=resettlement%20handbook, 28.

5. "UNHCR Global Trends: Forced Displacement in 2014," United Nations High Commissioner for Refugees, 2–3.

6. Ibid.

7. United Nations High Commissioner for Refugees, *UNHCR Resettlement Handbook*, 36.

8. "What We Do," United Nations High Commissioner for Refugees, http://www.unrefugees.org/what-we-do/.

9. "The 1972 Burundians," Center for Applied Linguistics, Cultural Orientation Resource Center, March 2007, http://www.rescue.org/sites/default/files/migrated/where/united_states_salt_lake_city_ut/1972-burundians-backgrounder-3-29-07.pdf.

10. In 2014, Tanzania did agree to offer citizenship to about two hundred thousand of the remaining Burundian refugees and their children who had fled their country in 1972, which serves as an example of local integration. See http://www.unhcr.org/544100746.html.

11. United Nations High Commissioner for Refugees, *UNHCR Resettlement Handbook*, 17.

12. Ibid., 37.

13. The other eight resettlement agencies are the US Conference of Catholic Bishops, Church World Service (affiliated with the National Council of Churches), the Lutheran Immigration and Refugee Service, Episcopal Migration Ministries, and the Hebrew Immigrant Aid Society (each of which is associated with a distinct religious tradition), as well as the International Rescue Committee, the US Committee for Refugees and Immigrants, and the Ethiopian Community Development Council (which are nonsectarian). See the Appendix for contact information for each of these agencies, as well as for World Relief's US offices.

14. Daniel C. Martin and James E. Yankay, "Annual Flow Report: Refugees and Asylees: 2013," US Department of Homeland Security Office of Immigration Statistics, August 2014, http://www.dhs.gov/sites/default/files/publications/ois_rfa_fr_2013.pdf, 4.

15. The per capita grant of $2,025 per refugee is accurate as of Fiscal Year 2016, but is subject to change.

16. "UNHCR Global Trends: Forced Displacement in 2014," United Nations High Commissioner for Refugees, 22.

17. Benjamin Bathke, "How Canada and the U.S. Compare on Syrian Refugees," Canadian Broadcasting Corporation, December 2, 2015, http://www.cbc.ca/news/canada/syrian-refugees-canada-united-states-comparison-1.3340852.

18. "Snapshot," Refugee Council of Australia, http://www.refugeecouncil.org.au/resources/statistics/snapshot/.

19. "Where Can I Obtain Humanitarian Settlement Services (HSS) Assistance?," Australian Government Department of Immigration and Citizenship, https://www.dss.gov.au/sites/default/files/documents/12_2013/hss_providers_booklet_access.pdf.

20. Tim Costello, "Australia's Humanity Is the Casualty of Repugnant Asylum Politics," World Vision Australia, August 16, 2013, https://www.worldvision.com.au/media-center/resource/australia's-humanity-is-the-casualty-of-repugnant-asylum-politics.

21. Pamela Duncan, "More than 1 Million People Have Sought EU Asylum So Far in 2015," *The Guardian,* December 9, 2015, http://www.theguardian.com/world/2015/dec/09/more-than-1-million-people-have-sought-eu-asylum-so-far-in-2015.

22. United Nations High Commissioner for Refugees, "EU Resettlement Fact Sheet," http://www.unhcr.org/524c31b69.html.

23. Christine Pohl, *Making Room: Recovering Hospitality as a Christian Tradition* (Grand Rapids: Eerdmans, 1999), 36.

24. Timothy Keller, *Generous Justice: How God's Grace Makes Us Just* (New York: Penguin, 2010), 52.

25. Soong-Chan Rah, Mission on Your Doorstep conference, Wheaton Bible Church, West Chicago, IL, March 5, 2010.

26. Jamie Dean, "Who Is My Neighbor?"

Chapter 6: Not (Quite) Refugees: Other Displaced People

1. Olivier Laurent, "Haiti Earthquake: Five Years Later," *TIME*, January 12, 2015, http://time.com/3662225/haiti-earthquake-five-year-after/.

2. Quoted in Scott Kraft, "Haitians Prepare for Boat Journey to Florida," *Los Angeles Times*, February 7, 2010, http://articles.latimes.com/2010/feb/07/world/la-fg-haiti-boats7-2010feb07.

3. Ibid. See also Joel Millman, "U.S. Lets Illegal Haitians Stay, Will Turn Back Refugees," *Wall Street Journal*, January 16, 2010, http://www.wsj.com/articles/SB10001424052748703657604575005233703955158; Russell Contreras, "Boston-Area Catholic Schools Welcome Haitian Refugees," *USA TODAY*, February 28, 2010, http://usatoday30.usatoday.com/news/religion/2010-04-28-haiti-catholic_N.htm; Laurie Ure, "U.S. Prepares Guantanamo Bay for Possible Influx of Haitians," CNN, January 21, 2010, http://www.cnn.com/2010/WORLD/americas/01/21/haiti.guantanamo/.

4. "Irregular Migrant, Refugee Arrivals in Europe Top One Million in 2015: IOM," International Organization for Migration, December 22, 2015, http://www.iom.int/news/irregular-migrant-refugee-arrivals-europe-top-one-million-2015-iom.

5. "How Many Migrants to Europe Are Refugees?," *The Economist*, September 7, 2015, http://www.economist.com/blogs/economist-explains/2015/09/economist-explains-4.

6. The term *immigrant* includes all those who have left their country to reside in another country, so refugees are a subcategory of immigrants, but not all immigrants are refugees—just as all Baptists fit within the larger category of Christians but not all Christians are Baptists.

7. Refugee Act of 1980 (Public Law 96-212), Title II, United States Government Printing Office, March 17, 1980, https://www.gpo.gov/fdsys/pkg/STATUTE-94/pdf/STATUTE-94-Pg102.pdf, bullet points added. The definition codified in US law by the Refugee Act is drawn from the language of the 1951 Convention Related to the Status of Refugees, which came in response to the

refugee crisis in Europe at the end of World War II, and which was expanded to include refugees from situations beyond that particular crisis by the 1967 Protocol Related to the Status of Refugees, to which 146 of the world's countries—including almost all European countries, Canada, Australia, and the United States—are parties.

8. The US legal definition of a refugee is slightly more flexible than the international definition in that, in particular "special circumstances" as determined by the president, refugee status can be designated to an individual who remains within their country of origin. The United States has applied this, in recent years, to particular individuals from Cuba, Iraq, and the former Soviet Union, and, very recently, to certain countries in Central America.

9. "Country Operations Profile: Syrian Arab Republic," United Nations High Commissioner for Refugees, June 2015, http://www.unhcr.org/pages/49e486a76.html.

10. "'Faithful, Do Not Leave Syria!': Patriarchs' Message, Rallied around the Pope," *Agenzia Fides*, September 14, 2012, http://www.fides.org/en/news/322 19?idnews=32219&lan=eng#.VoqWdPkrLLs.

11. Duncan, "More than 1 Million People Have Sought EU Asylum So Far in 2015."

12. Ted Robbins, "Little Known Immigration Mandate Keeps Detention Beds Full," NPR, November 19, 2013, http://www.npr.org/2013/11/19/245968601/little-known-immigration-mandate-keeps-detention-beds-full.

13. "Detained Asylum Seekers: Fiscal Year 2009 and 2010 Report to Congress," US Immigration and Customs Enforcement, August 20, 2012, https://www.ice.gov/doclib/foia/reports/detained-asylum-seekers2009-2010.pdf, 4, 8–9. Average time in detention is calculated by dividing the total number of nightly beds occupied by asylum seekers for Fiscal Year 2010 (1,233,286) divided by the total number of detained asylum seekers.

14. "Study: Private Prison Firms Spend Millions to Ensure Steady Supply of Undocumented Immigrants," Fox News Latino, April 21, 2015, http://latino .foxnews.com/latino/news/2015/04/21/private-prison-firms-spend-millions-to-ensure-steady-supply-of-undocumented-immigrants-study-says/.

15. Garance Burke and Laura Wides-Munoz, "Immigrants Prove Big Business for Prison Companies," Associated Press, August 2, 2012, http://news.yahoo .com/immigrants-prove-big-business-prison-companies-084353195.html.

16. "The Math of Immigration Detention," National Immigration Forum, August 2013, https://immigrationforum.org/wp-content/uploads/2014/10/Math-of-Immigation-Detention-August-2013-FINAL.pdf, 3.

17. Ivan Moreno, "Detained Immigrants Sue over Getting $1 Per Day for Work," Associated Press, July 10, 2015, http://bigstory.ap.org/article/9bd9c856a0874 5f68c151d7c1e2bf172/lawsuit-immigrants-got-1-day-work-private-prison.

18. Rex Dalton, "A Window into the World of Immigration Detainees," *The Voice of OC*, January 24, 2013, http://voiceofoc.org/2013/01/a-window-into-the-world-of-immigration-detainees/.

19. "Assessing the U.S. Government's Detention of Asylum Seekers," US Commission on International Religious Freedom, April 2013, http://www.uscirf. gov/sites/default/files/resources/ERS-detention%20reforms%20report%20 April%202013.pdf, 1.

20. "Immigration Detention: Additional Action Could Strengthen DHS Efforts to Address Sexual Abuse," US Government Accountability Office, November 2013, http://www.gao.gov/assets/660/659145.pdf.

21. "Lives in Peril: How Ineffective Inspections Make ICE Complicit in Immigration Detention Abuse," National Immigrant Justice Center and Detention Watch Network, October 2015, http://immigrantjustice.org/sites/immi-grantjusticc.org/files/THR-Inspections-FOIA-Report-October-2015-FINAL. pdf, 2.

22. Pastor Dantica's story is told in detail by his niece, Haitian-American novelist Edwidge Danticat, in *Brother, I'm Dying* (New York: Alfred A. Knopf, 2007).

23. "'At Least Let Them Work': The Denial of Work Authorization and Assistance for Asylum Seekers in the United States," Human Rights Watch, 2013, http:// www.rcusa.org/uploads/pdfs/us1113_asylum_forUPload.pdf.

24. Martin and Yankay, 6.

25. "FY 2014 Statistics Yearbook," US Department of Justice Executive Office for Immigration Review, March 2015, http://www.justice.gov/eoir/pages/attach ments/2015/03/16/fy14syb.pdf, K2.

26. Ibid., J1; Martin and Yankay, 5.

27. Kate M. Manuel, "Asylum and Gang Violence: Legal Overview," Congressional Research Service, September 5, 2014, https://www.fas.org/sgp/crs/homesec/ R43716.pdf, 17.

28. Based upon the US Department of State's February 2016 Visa Bulletin, family-based immigration petitions for a sibling of a US citizen from Mexico, which would also benefit the beneficiary's spouse and minor children, are currently being processed only from April 1, 1997, a backlog of approximately nineteen years.

29. Lauren Carasik, "Brutal Borders: Mexico's Immigration Crackdown—And How the United States Funds It," *Foreign Affairs*, November 4, 2015, https://www.foreignaffairs.com/articles/mexico/2015-11-04/brutal-borders.

30. "Children on the Run," United Nations High Commissioner for Refugees, July 2014, http://www.unhcrwashington.org/sites/default/files/1_UAC_Children%20on%20the%20Run_Full%20Report.pdf, 6.

31. Matthew Soerens, "How Churches Can Respond to the Unaccompanied Children Crisis," *Leadership Journal*, August 5, 2014, http://www.christianitytoday.com/le/2014/august-online-only/how-churches-can-respond-to-unaccompanied-children-crisis.html?paging=off.

32. Sonia Nazario, "The Children of the Drug Wars," *New York Times*, July 11, 2014, http://www.nytimes.com/2014/07/13/opinion/sunday/a-refugee-crisis-not-an-immigration-crisis.html.

33. "Representation for Unaccompanied Children in Immigration Court," Transactional Access Records Clearinghouse, Syracuse University, November 25, 2014, http://trac.syr.edu/immigration/reports/371/.

34. "El Salvador Becomes World's Most Deadly Country outside a War Zone," *The Telegraph*, January 5, 2015, http://www.telegraph.co.uk/news/worldnews/centralamericaandthecaribbean/elsalvador/12083903/El-Salvador-becomes-worlds-most-deadly-country-outside-a-war-zone.html.

35. Sibylla Brodzinsky and Ed Pilkington, "US Government Deporting Central American Migrants to Their Deaths," *The Guardian*, October 12, 2015, http://www.theguardian.com/us-news/2015/oct/12/obama-immigration-deportations-central-america.

36. Quoted in Cathy Lynn Grossman, "Rick Warren Speaks Up on Compassion, Politics, 'Big' Churches," *USA TODAY*, September 21, 2009, http://content.usatoday.com/communities/Religion/post/2009/09/rick-warren-lords-prayer-compassion-illegal-immigration/1#.Voy80_krLVY.

Chapter 7: The Church's Moment: Practical Opportunities to Respond

1. Tom Porter, "Refugee Crisis: Germany Has Received More than 1 Million Migrants in 2015," *International Business Times*, December 10, 2015, http://www.ibtimes.co.uk/refugee-crisis-germany-has-received-over-1-million-migrants-2015-1532674.

2. Randy Capps, Kathleen Newland et al, *The Integration Outcomes of U.S. Refugees* (Washington, DC: Migration Policy Institute, 2015), 11.

3. Tim Swarens, "The World Comes to Nora—for Christmas," *Indianapolis Star*, December 19, 2015, http://www.indystar.com/story/opinion/columnists/tim-swarens/2015/12/19/swarens-world-comes-nora-christmas/77553590/.

4. Alsegul Aydingun, Cigdem Balim Harding, Matthew Hoover, Igor Kuznet-zov, and Steve Swerdlow, *Meskhetian Turks: An Introduction to Their History, Culture, and Resettlement Practices* (Washington, DC: Center for Applied Linguistics, 2006).

5. Exceptions to the English language requirement can be made, in some cases, for those with particular medical disabilities, as certified by a physician, and for certain refugees who have been in the United States for at least fifteen years and are at least fifty-five years old or who are at least fifty years old and have resided in the country for at least twenty years.

6. "Changes in U.S. Family Finances from 2010 to 2013: Evidence from the Survey of Consumer Finances," *Federal Reserve Bulletin* 100, no. 4 (September 2014): 12. http://www.federalreserve.gov/pubs/bulletin/2014/pdf/scf14.pdf.

7. Thomas Boehm and Alan Schlottmann, "Does Home Ownership by Parents Have an Economic Impact on Their Children?," *Journal of Housing Economics* 8, no. 3 (September 1999): 228.

Chapter 8: Helping without Hurting: Understanding Challenges to Refugee Adjustment

1. Steve Corbett and Brian Fikkert, *When Helping Hurts: Alleviating Poverty without Hurting the Poor . . . and Yourself* (Chicago: Moody, 2009).

2. Thomas Elbert and Maggie Schauer, "Burnt into Memory," *Nature* 412 (2002): 883.

3. Thomas Elbert, Roland Weierstall, and Maggie Schauer, "Fascination Violence: On Mind and Brain of Man Hunters," *European Archives of Psychiatry and Clinical Neuroscience* 260, no. S2 (2010): 100–05.

4. Charles R. Figley, "Toward a Field of Traumatic Stress," *Journal of Traumatic Stress* 1, no. 1 (1988): 3–16.

5. Lars Weisaeth, "The European History of Psychotraumatology," *Journal of Traumatic Stress* 15, no. 6 (2002): 443–452.

6. United Nations High Commissioner for Refugees, *Resettlement Handbook* (2002), 236.

7. Alexander McFarlan, M. Atchison, E. Rafalowicz, and P. Papay, "Physical Symptoms in Post-traumatic Stress Disorder," *Journal of Psychosomatic Research* 38, no. 7 (1994): 715–26.

8. D. J. Somasundaram, *Child Trauma* (Jaffna: University of Jaffna, Sri Lanka, 1993); Ronald C. Kessler, "Posttraumatic Stress Disorder in the National Comorbidity Survey," *Archives of General Psychiatry* 52, no. 12 (1995): 1048–60.

9. *Diagnostic and Statistical Manual of Mental Disorders: DSM-5* (Washington, DC: American Psychiatric Association, 2013).

10. Chris R. Brewin, "A Cognitive Neuroscience Account of Posttraumatic Stress Disorder and Its Treatment," *Behaviour Research and Therapy* 39, no. 4 (2001): 373–93.

11. E. B. Foa et al., "Arousal, Numbing, and Intrusion: Symptom Structure of PTSD Following Assault," *American Journal of Psychiatry,* no. 152 (1995): 116–20.

12. Chris R. Brewin, Tim Dalgleish, and Stephen Joseph, "A Dual Representation Theory of Posttraumatic Stress Disorder," *Psychological Review* 103, no. 4 (1996): 670–86.

13. Larry R. Squire, "Declarative and Nondeclarative Memory: Multiple Brain Systems Supporting Learning and Memory," in D. L. Schacter & E. Tulving, eds., *Memory Systems* (Cambridge, MA: MIT Press, 1994), 207–28.

14. Anke Ehlers and David M. Clark, "A Cognitive Model of Posttraumatic Stress Disorder," *Behaviour Research and Therapy* 38, no. 4 (2000): 319–45.

15. Endel Tulving, "Episodic Memory and Common Sense: How Far Apart?" *Philosophical Transactions of the Royal Society B: Biological Sciences* 356, no. 1413 (2001): 1505–515.

16. P. J. Lang, "The network model of emotion: Motivational connections," in Thomas K. Srull and Robert S. Wyer, *Advances in Social Cognition* (Hillsdale, NJ: Lawrence Erlbaum Associate, 1993).

17. Treatments that have been effective include cognitive therapy, Narrative Exposure Therapy (NET), and Eye Movement Desensitization and Reprocessing (EMDR), among others.

18. Lisa McCann and Laurie Anne Pearlman, "Vicarious Traumatization: A Framework for Understanding the Psychological Effects of Working with Victims," *Journal of Traumatic Stress* 3 (1990): 1–5.

19. Stella Ting-Toomey, *Communicating across Cultures* (New York: Guilford, 1999), 10.

20. Gary R. Weaver, "Understanding and Coping with Cross-Cultural Adjustment Stress," in Gary R. Weaver, ed., *Culture, Communication and Conflict: Readings in Intercultural Relations* (New York: Simon & Schuster, 1998), 200.

21. C. G. Wrenn, "Afterword: The Culturally Encapsulated Counselor Revisited," in Paul Pedersen, *Handbook of Cross-Cultural Counseling and Therapy* (Westport, CT: Greenwood, 1985), 323–30.

22. Geert Hofstede, Gert Jan Hofstede, Michael Minkov, *Cultures and Organizations: Software of the Mind,* 3rd ed. (New York: McGraw-Hill USA, 2010), 90–91.

23. Ross Hammond and Robert Axelrod, "The Evolution of Ethnocentrism," *Journal of Conflict Resolution* 50, no. 6 (December 2006): 1.

24. Cited in Karen South Moustafa, "Differences in the Use of Media across Cultures," *Encyclopedia of Virtual Communities and Technologies,* ed. Subhasish Dasgupta (Hershey, PA· Idea Group, 2006), 131.

25. M. R. Hammer, "The Intercultural Conflict Style Inventory: A Conceptual Framework and Measure of Intercultural Conflict Approaches," *International Journal of Intercultural Research 29* (2005): 675–95.

26. Ibid.

27. *Making Your Way: A Reception and Placement Orientation Curriculum* (Washington, DC: Cultural Orientation Resource Center, 2013).

28. Matthew Nelson, Julia Meredith Hess, Brian Isakson, and Jessica Goodkind, "Seeing the Life: Redefining Self-Worth and Family Roles among Iraqi Refugee Families Resettled in the United States," *Journal of International Migration and Integration* (2015): 1–16.

29. Psychologists refer to this as a "corrective emotional experience." See F. Alexander, "Zur Genese des Kastrationskomplexes," *Internationale Zeitschift für Psychoanalyse* XVI Band (1930), (English transl. by C. F. Menninger, "Concerning the Genesis of the Castration Complex," *Psychoanalytic Review* XXII [1935]: 1.)

Chapter 9: Root Causes: Responding to the Larger Issues That Compel People to Flee

1. "UNHCR Global Trends: Forced Displacement in 2014," United Nations High Commissioner for Refugees.

2. Elena Fiddian-Qasmiyeh et al., *The Oxford Handbook of Refugee and Forced Migration Studies* (Oxford: Oxford University Press, August 24, 2014), Kindle location 8258–360.

3. Susan Martin et al., *Humanitarian Crises and Migration: Causes, Consequences and Responses* (New York: Routledge, 2014), Kindle location 427.

4. Olivier Laurent, "Haiti Earthquake: Five Years Later."

5. US Geological Survey, "Earthquake Information for 2010," October 30, 2012, http://earthquake.usgs.gov/earthquakes/eqarchives/year/2010/.

6. Mark Thiessen, "Magnitude-7.1 Quake Jolts Alaska; 4 Homes Lost," Associated Press, January 24, 2016, http://bigstory.ap.org/article/3c51faed18ce46b68c4cb 7d889a5ae20/federal-agency-magnitude-64-earthquake-hit-southern-alaska.

7. Susan Martin et al., *Humanitarian Crises and Migration: Causes, Consequences and Responses*, Kindle location 8350.

8. Paul Hiebert, *Transforming Worldviews: An Anthropological Understanding of How People Change* (Grand Rapids: Baker, 2008), Kindle location 501.

9. Yale University Genocide Studies Program, "Cambodian Genocide Program," http://gsp.yale.edu/case-studies/cambodian-genocide-program.

10. Corbett and Fikkert, *When Helping Hurts*, 53.

11. Deepa Narayan, *Voices of the Poor: Can Anyone Hear Us?* (Oxford: Oxford University Press, 2002), 2.

12. Bryant Myers, *Walking with the Poor* (Maryknoll, NY: Orbis, 1999), 76.

13. "Syria Refugees: UN Warns of Extreme Poverty in Jordan," British Broadcasting Corporation, January 14, 2015, http://www.bbc.com/news/world-middle-east-30815084.

14. "48 Women Raped Every Hour in Congo, Study Finds," CBS News, May 11, 2011, http://www.cbsnews.com/news/48-women-raped-every-hour-in-congo-study-finds/.

15. Heather Harvey, "Rape Is Cheaper than Bullets," *The Guardian*, February 24, 2009, http://www.theguardian.com/commentisfree/2009/feb/24/warcrimes-congo.

16. Nicholas D. Kristof and Sheryl WuDunn, *Half the Sky: Turning Oppression into Opportunity for Women Worldwide* (New York: Alfred A. Knopf, 2009), 86.

17. Ibid., 109.

18. Keller, *Generous Justice*, 10.

19. Nicholas Wolterstorff, *Justice: Rights and Wrongs* (Princeton, NJ: Princeton University Press, 2007), Kindle location 55.

20. Take, for example, Jesus' mandate in Luke 4:18–19: "The Spirit of the Lord is on me, because he has anointed me to proclaim good news to the poor. He has sent me to proclaim freedom for the prisoners and recovery of sight for the blind, to set the oppressed free, to proclaim the year of the Lord's favor."

21. Stephan addresses these dynamics of global poverty and injustice in more depth in *Possible: A Blueprint for Changing How We Change the World* (Portland, OR: Multnomah, 2015).

22. US State Department Bureau of Democracy, Human Rights, and Labor, "Cambodia," *International Religious Freedom Report 2007*, http://go.usa.gov/3pHwh.

Chapter 10: Confronting Injustice: Why Policy Matters

1. Mike Lanchin, "*SS St Louis*: The Ship of Jewish Refugees No One Wanted," *BBC World Service*, May 13, 2014, http://www.bbc.com/news/magazine-27373131.

2. Rafael Medoff, "Anne Frank Was Barred, but Her Tree Made It to the U.S.," *Arutz Sheva*, April 7, 2013, http://www.israelnationalnews.com/Articles/Article.aspx/13103#.VpbIfvkrLVZ.

3. Ibid.

4. Noel Castellanos, *Where the Cross Meets the Street: What Happens to the Neighborhood When God Is at the Center* (Downers Grove, IL: InterVarsity, 2015), 136.

5. Alexa Ura, "Halt All Refugee Resettlement, Two Texas Congressmen Say," *Texas Tribune*, November 18, 2015, http://www.texastribune.org/2015/11/18/two-texas-congressmen-want-stop-all-refugee-resett/.

6. Martin Luther King Jr., "Beyond Vietnam," April 4, 1967, http://kingencyclopedia.stanford.edu/kingweb/publications/speeches/Beyond_Vietnam.pdf, 9.

7. Tim Keller, "The Beauty of Biblical Justice," *By Faith*, October 26, 2010, http://byfaithonline.com/the-beauty-of-biblical-justice/.

8. Amy E. Black, "The Cure for Election Madness: How to Be Political without Losing Your Soul," *Christianity Today*, January 6, 2012, http://www.christianitytoday.com/ct/2012/january/election-madness.html?share=2PzPL0AwlYH9zOrD7BfFLCt4EM4UlW17. For more information on this topic, see Amy Black, *Honoring God in Red or Blue: Approaching Politics with Humility, Grace, and Reason* (Chicago: Moody, 2012).

9. By taking in a slightly larger share of the globe's refugees, the US government would also have increased credibility in its diplomatic efforts to persuade other countries—some of which are hosting a far larger number of refugees and asylum seekers—to do more as well.

10. "A Christian Declaration on Caring for Refugees: An Evangelical Response," GC2 Summit, December 17, 2015, http://www.gc2summit.com/statement/.

11. "Letter to Members of Congress," Evangelical Immigration Table, December 2, 2015, http://evangelicalimmigrationtable.com/cms/assets/uploads/2015/12/EIT-Syrian-refugee-letter.pdf.

12. "Letter to Senators Durbin and Kirk," Evangelical Immigration Table, December 17, 2015, http://evangelicalimmigrationtable.com/cms/assets/uploads/2015/12/Dec-2015-IL-Pastors-Letter-on-Refugees.pdf.

13. Alexia Salvatierra and Peter Heltzel, *Faith-Rooted Organizing: Mobilizing the Church in Service to the World* (Downers Grove, IL: InterVarsity, 2014), 111.

14. Russell Moore, "Stop Pitting Security and Compassion against Each Other in the Syrian Refugee Crisis," *Washington Post*, November 19, 2015, https://www.washingtonpost.com/news/acts-of-faith/wp/2015/11/19/stop-pitting-security-and-compassion-against-each-other-in-the-syrian-refugee-crisis/.

15. Quoted in Diane Smith, "Syrian Refugees: DFW Clergy Weigh in on What Jesus Would Do," *Fort Worth Star-Telegram*, November 20, 2015, http://www.star-telegram.com/news/local/community/fort-worth/article45607614.html.

16. Jonathan Serrie, "Popular Georgia Evangelical Pastor Criticized Anti-Refugee Politics," Fox News, December 21, 2015, http://www.foxnews.com/us/2015/12/21/popular-georgia-evangelical-pastor-criticizes-anti-refugee-politics.html.

Chapter 11: "A Shining City on a Hill"

1. Ronald Reagan, "Farewell Address to the Nation," January 11, 1989, http://www.reagan.utexas.edu/archives/speeches/1989/011189i.htm.

2. Emma Lazarus, "The New Colossus," in *Selected Poems*, ed. John Hollander (New York: Library of America, 2005), 58.

3. "Mixed Views of Initial US Response to Europe's Migrant Crisis," Pew Research Center, September 29, 2015, http://www.people-press.org/2015/09/29/mixed-views-of-initial-u-s-response-to-europes-migrant-crisis/.

4. "Pastor Views on Refugees," LifeWay Research.

5. Ibid.

ACKNOWLEDGMENTS

Our World Relief colleagues—where we're physically present most often, in Baltimore, Maryland, and in Wheaton and Aurora, Illinois, respectively, but also at all of our other locations throughout the world—have been a remarkable help in supporting this book project. Special thanks, in particular, to colaborers in Spokane, Garden Grove, Jacksonville, Seattle, Sacramento, Modesto, Memphis, Spartanburg, Durham, High Point, Berlin, Amman, and Phnom Penh who helped us track down stories and verify facts. From caseworkers to church mobilizers to administrative, marketing, and human resources support staff, they collectively do the work day in and day out of serving refugees and other vulnerable people alongside local churches. We're grateful that all the proceeds from this book's sales can go right back into our mission of empowering local churches to serve the vulnerable, and for the many supporting churches and donors who sustain this work.

Various of our colleagues, as well as some friends outside of World Relief, reviewed, fact-checked, and edited this manuscript (though any remaining errors are our responsibility). Thanks especially to Jenny Yang, James Misner, Dan Kosten, Susan Sperry, Emily Gray, Andrew Timbie, Mandy Barb, Casey Leyva, Galen Carey at the National Association of Evangelicals, Pat Hatch with the Presbyterian Church of America's Mission to North America, and Tara Peters at the University of Chicago's Pozen Family Center for Human Rights. Our Wheaton College student intern, Leela Kim, helped cheerfully with the tedious work of formatting this manuscript and tracking down citations. Don Jacobson very graciously offered his considerable talents to help find a home for this project with Moody Publishers.

Bill and Lynne Hybels have been friends to each of us in different settings over the years, and we were thrilled that they agreed to write the foreword to this book. Time after time, they have followed Jesus in standing for those who are vulnerable, even when that has meant leading people into new and uncomfortable territory.

This book wouldn't have made it into your hands (or onto your e-reader, as the case may be) without the incredible team at Moody Publishers, who had the vision for this project before we did. Thanks, especially, to Duane Sherman and Randall Payleitner for believing in this effort and championing it through to completion. Ginger Kolbaba has a God-given gift for editing and wordsmithing and rightfully insisted that we couldn't use the expression "missional opportunity" four times in the same paragraph. And the marketing teams at both Moody and World Relief probably have a lot to do with this book landing in your hands.

Our friends and colleagues working with the Evangelical Immigration Table—past and present, from the field team up to the Table's principals—have modeled how followers of Jesus can come together to stand for just public policies. Vickie Reddy and the folks at We Welcome Refugees have built a similar coalition in support of the displaced. We're grateful.

Stephan Bauman
My wholehearted thanks to those who helped make this book possible. First and foremost, to the millions of people we call refugees but who are, in the end, sojourners from whom we have so much to

learn; to Matthew Soerens for giving unconditionally to this project and leading us so well; to Issam Smeir for joining us in a project we could not have done alone; to Duane Sherman and the team at Moody Publishers and Don Jacobson and Marty Raz at Zeal Books for visioning this project with us; to Belinda, Joshua, and Caleb for loving those who sojourn as we learn to do the same ourselves: my love is all yours.

Issam Smeir

I would like to acknowledge a few people who were instrumental in encouraging me throughout this project. First, my wife, Stephanie Mumford Smeir. She proves the truth of the old wise saying that "a man should never be afraid to marry a woman who is smarter than he is." We met twelve years ago at a fundraising event, when she was running a residential program in Chicago for severely neglected and abused children. She spoke for a few minutes at the event, and that was more than enough to steal my heart for eternity. Her passion for justice issues lifted my spirit and has allowed me to spend months every year away from home working with refugees and victims of torture in the Middle East and North Africa.

Second, I am indebted to Matthew Soerens, who recruited me to join him and Stephan to write this book. His advice, suggestions, and input were instrumental for me throughout this project. Richard Stellway reviewed and edited portions of the manuscript and offered valuable advice about various ideas and concepts. His prayers and words of encouragement about my work in the Middle East tremendously helped me to keep going. Gary R. Collins is my mentor who has taken me under his wing over the years and treated me like his own son.

I am also thankful to the World Relief DuPage staff, particularly

Emily Gray, Liliana Popovic, and Susan Sperry, who were excited about this project since its conception. They all worked with me so I could take the necessary time away from my daily duties with clients to join and participate in this project.

And finally, for the four bundles of joy in my life: Laith, Liam, Luke, and Zain. You are the first people whom I think of in the morning and the last people I pray for at the end of my day. Thanks for interrupting me consistently while writing this book, reminding me that there are more important things in life than writing and working.

Matthew Soerens
Two decisions about ten years ago made my involvement in this book possible: accepting a job at World Relief DuPage and moving into the Parkside Apartments in Glen Ellyn, Illinois.

To each of my neighbors at Parkside over the years, most of them refugees or other immigrants: thank you. Living among you was the most profound experience of neighborhood and community I've had, and I fear I'll never experience anything quite like it again. Thanks, especially, to Janvier, Marie Josée, Mireille, Christian, Ricka, and Daniella; Inocencia Escobar, Irving Ruiz, and Areli Ruiz; Celia Culebrina and family; Marie Claire and Celestin and family; Roque, Teresa, Karen, and Jovani Garcia; Nyakir Deng and Tom Awan; Wani Suliman and family; Pascal and Lydie Atchrimi; Dominique Atchrimi; Mama Adjoua; Joseph and Ellen Dahnweih; Ah Na and family; Peiman Khamisi; Renbow Danh; Pascal Ramadhani; Ryan Himes, Ben Lowe, Josh Martin, Jonathan Kindberg, Sado Park, Aaron Fisher, Nathan Liu, Kags Ndethiu, Maria Mulhauser, David and Christy Vosburg, Betsy and Mark Hinsch, Luke and Shannon Niermann, Jason Ahlenius, Jacob Rodriguez, Theogene Nishimwe,

John Raines, Chris Wilson, Ellen Leahy, and Liz Dong.

In Aurora, where we live now, I've been well supported both in prayer and in all sorts of tangible ways by friends at Community Christian Church's East Aurora Campus—especially Obe and Jack Arellano, Kirsten and Scott Strand, Victor and Poliana Negreiros, Eric and Kelly Stade, Josue and Maria Mata, Omar Ornelas, Daisy Ornelas, Suzy Menchaca, and Rafael Menchaca. Our upstairs neighbors for a season, Saeed, Hameedah, and Salwan, became dear friends during the year they lived above us.

When I asked my wife, Diana, what she thought of the idea of me and a few colleagues producing a book in a little more than a month, her response, as it has been to any number of crazy ideas, was, "Let's do it." And I couldn't have done it without you. I love you so much.

Finally, Zipporah and Zephaniah: being your dad is the greatest privilege I can imagine. I love you.

WE'VE SEEN THE NEWS.

WE'VE HEARD THE STORIES.

**BUT MANY OF US QUESTION WHETHER
THERE'S ANYTHING WE CAN DO.**

THE ANSWER - THERE IS.

EACH OF US HAS THE OPPORTUNITY TO
UNLOCK HOPE FOR THOSE
WE'VE HEARD SO MUCH ABOUT.

MAKE A DIFFERENCE:
worldrelief.org/unlockhope

UNLOCK H⦿PE
world relief

HOW TO HELP

For practical next steps and ways to
proactively engage in the refugee crisis,
visit *worldrelief.org/seekingrefuge*
where you'll find ways to:

 Form a Good Neighbor Team at your
local church to welcome and walk
alongside a newly arrived refugee
family in your community.

 Put together Welcome Kits containing
the basic items that a newly arrived
refugee family will need as they rebuild
their lives in the United States.

world relief™

worldrelief.org

f 🞀 🐦 ⱱ

Send an email to your elected officials, urging them to pursue more welcoming refugee policies.

 Through **Unlock Hope** you can financially support World Relief's work with local partners serving refugees in the Middle East, Europe, and the US.

The mission of World Relief is to empower the local church to serve the most vulnerable. We live this out by partnering with local churches in the United States and abroad to bring wholistic transformation to communities.

In the US, we partner with both the US State Department and thousands of local churches to resettle refugees in more than 25 communities throughout the country. Globally—in the Middle East, Africa, Asia, and beyond—we equip local churches both to meet the immediate needs of displaced people and to address the root causes of poverty, conflict, and injustice that fuel refugee crises.

We invite you to join us as at worldrelief.org as we stand for the vulnerable.

world relief™

worldrelief.org

f 🖸 🐦 𝑣

NOW IS THE CHURCH'S TIME TO RESPOND.

Equip yourself with sermon notes, FAQs, myths & facts, and an infographic on the US refugee screening process.

Download your free copy of our practical guide, A Church Leader's Tool Kit to the Syrian Refugee Crisis.

Visit refugeecrisis.worldrelief.org/church-resources/ to download today.

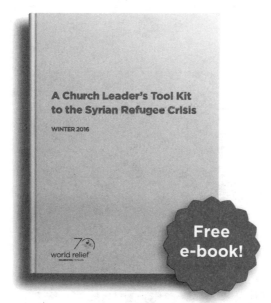

world relief™

worldrelief.org

f ⌾ 🐦 𝓋

FOLLOW US!

Follow us on social media to
stay up to speed on news regarding
the current refugee crisis and how
you can help in your area.

@WORLDRELIEF

world relief™

worldrelief.org

GOOD INTENTIONS ARE NOT ENOUGH.

Keep exploring how you and your church can foster lasting transformation in the lives of the materially poor.

WHEN HELPING HURTS

Explore the foundational concepts, principles, and strategies.

WHEN HELPING HURTS: THE SMALL GROUP EXPERIENCE

What does it look like to explore poverty alleviation as a group?

HELPING WITHOUT HURTING IN SHORT-TERM MISSIONS: LEADER'S GUIDE

How do I lead a short-term mission trip well?

HELPING WITHOUT HURTING IN SHORT-TERM MISSIONS: PARTICIPANT'S GUIDE

How can I be as prepared as possible for my next mission trip?

HELPING WITHOUT HURTING IN CHURCH BENEVOLENCE

What should my church do when someone asks for financial help?

Everyone is born with God-given creativity waiting to be unleashed.

To succeed today we simply must add creativity to our toolbox. With how fast the world is changing, today's methods will soon be outdated. What we need for tomorrow is the ability to adapt and innovate, and to inspire the same in others.

createvs.copy will equip you to do just that. Exploring the theory and practice of creativity, imagination, and innovation, Ken Wytsma shows you how to:

- **Cultivate a creative mindset in life and leadership**
- **Approach problem solving with greater imagination**
- **Rediscover why you do what you do and how to do it better**

Also available as an ebook

 moody collective

 MOODY Publishers™

MOODYCOLLECTIVE.COM